THE LIE THAT SETTLES

THE LIE THAT SETTLES

A MEMOIR

PETER FARRELL

For Marion (1899–1964).
A pioneer in her own way.

2013
© Peter Farrell

The author gratefully acknowledges the support
of Mission Hall Creative.
Typeset by Mission Hall Creative.

Cover photograph: Bike ride around the grounds at Redhill 1950.

ISBN 978-0-473-29343-7

PETONE PUBLISHING

www.theliethatsettles.com
www.petonepublishing.com

CONTENTS

1947: Near Maidstone, Kent, England

The seasons in the countryside could be measured by the hop vines as they crept up the wires. It was autumn now, and the vines were full. The air outside the cone-shaped oast houses shimmered with the heat from the furnaces and there was an acrid smell of drying hops. Each year the hop-pickers arrived from bomb-scarred London for a brief working holiday. City coexisted uneasily with the country for the two or three weeks it took the visitors to strip the vines by hand and create chaos in the surrounding Kentish villages.

Wednesday was Mum's half day off. That day was no different from others. We trudged up the hill, past the oast houses. We always caught the 10.30am number 12A green and yellow bus to Maidstone. She stooped slightly to catch my chatter. My small warm hand snuggled into hers and she must have been aware of me fingering her wedding band. She was then in her late forties and I was seven years old. Despite my age we talked about everything, from the previous night's wireless programmes to the latest misdemeanours of the government. People had been moaning about the havoc that was being caused by the hop-pickers. Mum said it wasn't fair, Londoners had put up with a lot during the Blitz. She should know, because she was born in the East End.

We arrived early at the bus stop. Waiting for the bus was part of the Wednesday ritual. I sat astride the milestone waiting, my short legs swinging. My fingers picked over the strange eighteenth century lettering chiselled into the stone as I wondered about highwaymen and stagecoaches.

Then there was the distant sound of a diesel engine. I liked to stand in the middle of the road looking out for the green top of the bus above the hedgerows as it picked its way towards us. The bus driver nodded to us as he slowed down. I always went upstairs at the front of the bus, above the driver's cab where I could get a driver's eye view of the road ahead for the thirty minutes or so it took us to get to town. Mum liked it upstairs too because she could smoke. Her face was drawn and lined, grey hair pulled back in a bun. It was her day off so she wore her dark blue coat with its padded shoulders and large buttons up the front. Its cut was not quite the style that prevailed, but it was still worn with some panache. There was a presence about her slight body that age could not erode. She drew deeply on the cigarette and blew smoke out with a satisfied sigh.

When we got to the bus station in Maidstone I asked if we could stay and watch the buses for a bit. She nodded her agreement. We always had plenty of time and were easy in one another's company. She got a cup of tea from the bus station café, and we watched the buses arriving and departing, some to exotic destinations like Canterbury, Hastings and even London.

The man in the stationer's in the High Street saw us coming and reached below the counter for our regular order. He pushed over a comic for me, and the *Kent Messenger* for Mum, together with her usual packet of Player's Weights cigarettes. We wandered down the High Street to the Cannon Restaurant. A cardboard notice flapped on the door – *No hop-pickers or gypsies served here.* Squeezing into a seat by the window, she lit up her Player's as she checked the paper to see what was on at the Granada. The film that day was *The Fallen Idol.* It was A-rated, so the pictures were out of the question. We'd have to make do with fish and chips and a cup of tea instead. I liked going to the pictures, but it was cosy in the Cannon. She looked over the paper, reading extracts to me although I wasn't really listening. I lost myself in the world of comic book heroes.

"It says in here that a lot of people who were thought to be dead have really been alive all the time." I traced the illustrations and text in the comic in front of me. Then I added, "There's a story here about some Jap soldiers who've just been found in the jungle and the war's been over for two years now. Perhaps my dad is out there somewhere. How did you say he was killed?"

If she hesitated, I did not notice it. She reached over and ruffled my thick curly black hair.

"Don't you remember me telling you?" She reached into her handbag, scrabbling around for another Player's. "He was a teacher. He was getting his class into a shelter during an air raid and was outside when the bomb hit. He was looking for a boy who was lost. It was a very brave thing to do."

I quite liked having a hero for a father, although I would have preferred him to have been a Spitfire pilot. I didn't miss him at all. Lots of kids had lost a father in the war.

I returned my attention to my comic. We could have been an old married couple.

1994: Wellington, New Zealand

Dear Morris

This letter is going to be as difficult for me to write as it will be for you to read…

You may or may not have wondered what happened to your son, Peter, who was born in 1940. My mother was Marion Farrell. I know you will have heard through Shaw of her death and my subsequent departure to New Zealand in 1965. I can fill in the gaps for you if that is what you want but I hesitate to give you the full autobiography in case it causes anxiety.

I have, for both our sakes, thought hard about making contact. I have decided to do so now because I think we have reached stages in our lives when we can establish some sort of basis for communication. For me, it would help me understand and come to terms with a part of my life I can only speculate about. I cannot anticipate what such contact will mean for you but I hope you will see it as an opportunity to know a little about this person with whom you are so intimately involved. I know that you married and had another son and a daughter. I have no wish to cause them unease and have had to come to terms with the fact that they may not know of my existence.

I hope you will respond soon to these stumbling words. Whatever you decide to do, I want you to know that this letter is about reconciliation and understanding. I am endlessly grateful to you for the life you gave me all those years ago.

Your son
Peter

PART 1
MARION

1

EAST END LIFE

My grandmother Mary Richardson married an Irish house painter called Thomas Farrell in 1887. Family folklore had it that she married beneath herself. Thomas seems to have contributed very little beyond fathering thirteen children. Of these, the first, Nell, and the last, Freddie, died of TB a few years after their birth. My mother, Marion, was the seventh, born in 1899.

Marion's birth was remarkable only for the fact that it was the last birth at which both mother and father were present. For the later six confinements, the older sisters, Mary Ann and Agnes, cared for their mother and did whatever else was needed. Thomas found his wife's pregnancies unsettling and used to take off to his own mother to be looked after when the birth of a child drew near. Marion seldom mentioned her father to me and when she did, it was to dismiss him as an irrelevance, a drinker and a burden to them all. He died, an apparently unlamented death, in 1911.

Pictures of Mary Farrell as a young woman show a delicate, prim figure, but by the time she reached her eighties she was heavy and careworn. With up to eight growing children in the house at any one time, someone had to take charge and provide care and discipline in the household. Mary's role as the matriarch was accepted, and all of her children spoke with great affection of their mother and the unfussy way she went about her work. She hid behind a dark cockney wit. She was fiercely protective of her children and how the world might perceive them. Their secrets were safe with her.

They moved to Barrington Road in 1913. You can still walk from there, through the smoke-darkened and eerie railway arches, to East Ham Station. The fog no longer swirls around and rag and bone merchants don't push their carts as they did when the Farrell family moved in. The domino clattering of goods wagons being reorganised in the marshalling yards has been replaced by the aggressive hum of diesels as they hurry by to exotic cross-channel destinations.

In 1913, the only feature distinguishing 32 Barrington Road from its terraced neighbours was its number. The front door opened into a narrow passage with stairs leading up to two bedrooms, and a box room the size of a large cupboard. Downstairs, each house had a small kitchen and a back parlour with a black stove. The front room was the focal point for special occasions. At 32, one of the Farrell boys had painted a blue, moonlit scene from the Arabian Nights, which covered all four walls. The artist was probably Tommy, who had seen out some of the war in a mysterious part of the world. The mural was an elaborate piece of work and provided an exotic backdrop on bath night when the tin bath was filled up in front of the fire. Outside, there was a toilet and a small vegetable garden backing onto the railway lines.

By the time the family moved to Barrington Road all the talk was of war with Germany. The Great War lasted from 1914 to 1918.

Marion left school at fifteen years old. Available documentation shows her as suitable for 'shop work', which was a step up from factory work. School had been a struggle for her. Naturally left-handed, she had been forced to hold crayons and pencils with her right hand. Her signature on the documentation is blotched and uncertain, but perhaps it would eventually be her ticket out of Barrington Road.

She had no intention of working in a shop. There was a shortage of labour in the munitions factories, and some of the leading and formerly militant suffragettes ran a patriotic campaign on behalf of the government to enlist women for the work. Recruitment booths were set up all over the East End. To Marion, this seemed more exciting and useful than shop work. She signed on at the booth at East Ham underground station, joining her older sister Agnes, who was already working at the Royal Arsenal at Woolwich. Munitions assembly was dangerous work. A few of the girls who weren't so careful with handling the chemicals ended up with faces stained bright yellow. These 'canaries', as they were called, were withdrawn from the factory as soon as the condition appeared. There were also tales of vomiting, delirium and loss of sight that frequently followed the breathing in of the fumes. The girls talked and they knew that some canaries never recovered their senses. Some died in sweat-damp beds in streets like Barrington Road. Each day the two sisters came home, arm in arm, hoarse from shouting above the screech of machinery, hands stained from the ammunition.

By 1915, the neighbours' boys were beginning to return from the Front. A few could be seen wandering the streets propped up on flimsy crutches, with wide blank stares fixed upon some distant horizon. Others, still waiting to be sent away, came to call, looking to establish their manhood before disappearing across the Channel. One or two may have misinterpreted Marion's slight body, the laughing eyes and delicately boned face as some sign of weakness, promising an easy conquest. She enjoyed the repartee, the flirting and the dancing but there was some predictability to it all that made her uneasy. She couldn't understand why these young men were so happy to go off to the war when it was already becoming obvious that so many of them would not return. Conscription was introduced in 1916.

There were few men at the factory so Marion soon noticed a group of young men always huddled together smoking during tea breaks. They looked strong and fit but their faces were old and tired, with wary, hooded eyes. She wondered why nobody talked to them. Agnes was contemptuous. They were conchies. White-feather men. "Won't go to the war. Bunch of cowards if you ask me. Bolsheviks most of 'em," she said in her dismissive way.

Marion wasn't prepared to dismiss this group quite so easily. She never risked sitting with them but always made a point from then on of smiling and acknowledging their presence. Sometimes one or two would smile back. Agnes didn't approve but then she very rarely understood the things Marion did and why she did them.

One day Marion found a pamphlet pushed into her apron as she was leaving the canteen. The paper was crumpled and the printing ink had smeared. Workers, according to what was written there, were being sacrificed needlessly in the trenches to preserve the lifestyle of the landowning classes. It was a capitalist's war. The paper contained a contact address in East Ham, with a date and time for a meeting in a local hall. Marion decided to go along. She didn't tell her sisters where she was going. She was curious, excited and afraid. Pacifism was a dangerous notion to have in Barrington Road in those days, and she knew that her family would have no sympathy for the conchies any more than they had for Sylvia Pankhurst and that lot of crazy women.

The gathering in East Ham was like an evangelical meeting. Speakers shook their fists at perceived evils and fantasised about a promised land where everyone was equal. There were more women there than she'd expected, although she didn't see many factory headscarves in evidence. Most of the women wore hats, secured with jewelled hatpins. There was talk of war as an obscenity rather than a patriotic duty. Some speakers questioned why young men were dying across the Channel and whether their deaths would achieve anything for the working class. Marion sat quietly, in awe of the risky, unpatriotic things that were being said, afraid to interrupt the passionate flow of rhetoric. She became deeply aware of her lack of learning, her raw East End vowels and, worst of all, where she worked.

One young speaker, struggling to keep his voice from squeaking an octave higher, announced with self-conscious bravado, "If I am to be labelled a conchie and sent to Wormwood Scrubs then so be it!"

Marion knew what would probably happen to this young chap if he refused conscription. He'd be safer in Wormwood Scrubs than on the streets of East Ham.

If some of these people were to be believed, munitions workers were simply a tool of an evil arms industry that was profiteering from the war. Marion had never heard criticism of the upper classes before, even within her family. Her mother did not trust those who had the right to rule but had always been resigned to her place in the world.

Bolsheviks, Socialists, Quakers, there were so many viewpoints on offer at that first meeting. Sometimes Marion would be swayed by the Socialists, who were full of spitting anger, but then a Quaker would stand up and speak with serenity and certainty about the sanctity of human life. It was all very seductive. She continued to attend meetings in the smoky halls or grubby attic rooms in different parts of the East End. She started to tell the family as much as she felt they needed to know about the meetings she attended.

Marion was a follower rather than a leader and her mother worried what particular leader she would latch on to. Perhaps there was a candidate amongst some of the strange young men she had brought home from her meetings. One or two of them had the gift of the gab and Marion seemed to admire that.

The conflict of working in a munitions factory during the day and attending pacifist meetings at night became too much for Marion. Some of the women who went to the meetings had been to the Front, driving lorries or nursing, but you needed qualifications and skills for those jobs. Marion found life at Barrington Road too constricting but she was still only seventeen years old. Her mother would not countenance her leaving home unless it was into a job where accommodation was provided. At one of the Socialist meetings she heard about the Women's Land Army, which had been recently set up to recruit women onto the land, covering for farm labourers who had been sent to the war. This could be a way out for her, she thought.

By Marion's account, the interview for the Women's Land Army was conducted by a ruddy-faced, square woman. The woman had dark, short hair, peppered grey. Dandruff settled on the collar of her serge jacket. Two boxer dogs slept under the table while she walked back and forth slapping her jodhpurs with worn leather gloves to emphasise a point.

"We are looking for gels with good moral character, go to church and all that sort of thing, eh?" The staccato voice had the air of a head prefect about it. There was a slight glistening of sweat caught in the down of her upper lip. "The work is hard so it's no good taking it on if all you are interested in is wearing breeches and powdering your nose. Pretty gels are no use to us," she said contemptuously. "We want good workers. You can't be a pretty gel and a good worker. Understand?"

"I learned to play the piano at Sunday School and still go to church when I can." Marion had lied on the second point. If they were anything the Farrells were Catholic, but it was not a strong allegiance. "At the factory we have to do all the work that men do so I'm sure you won't be disappointed." She didn't know what to say about being pretty so she didn't mention that.

Neither the month's training she was given in the Women's Land Army nor the written material provided was very specific about the work she would be doing, but both were very strong on retaining high moral standards. The wording in the handbook caused a few giggles amongst the cockney girls who knew all about the controversy surrounding the kitting out of Land Army girls in breeches, then regarded as synonymous with sexual depravity:

You are doing a man's work and so you are dressed rather like a man; but remember that just because you wear a smock and breeches you should take care to behave like an English girl who expects chivalry and respect from everyone she meets. Noisy or ugly behaviour brings discredit, not only on yourself but upon the uniform, and the whole Women's Land Army. When people see you pass…show them an English girl who is working for her country on the land is the best sort of girl.[1]

Marion was assigned to a farm near Chelmsford, about thirty

---

1 *The Countryside at War* – Dakers, Caroline.

miles east of London. She liked the uniform, the trousers and the racy messages it sent about its wearers. She learned a lot about farm work and became interested in growing nutritious produce. The farmer, like many at the time, had to be persuaded that having women working for him was a good idea but he was welcoming in his gruff way. The male farmhands he employed had been too old for call-up. One or two thought they would have a bit of fun with the new recruit from London. They were mistaken. Marion was not ready for those sorts of adventures. She learned to use her sharp wit and sharper tongue to talk herself out of threatening situations. She found that swearing with imagination and vigour soon scared off invaders who had never heard the like from such a young woman.

The end of the war was an anticlimax for Marion. Farm workers were returning from the Front and the Women's Land Army was being wound down. In November 1918, the church bells in the village rang in a peal as if someone was getting married. Marion was allowed off the farm to go to the Armistice Day service. A few days later they were bussed into Chelmsford where some lady from London presented them with their Women's Land Army service badges.

At Barrington Road, her mother turned over the service badge in her gnarled red hands, while Marion talked to her about life in the country.

"I knew you'd want to leave home when you got back from the Land Army. You needn't worry about buttering me up and getting me ready for it." The older woman smiled tightly. Marion's mother had the knack of being one step ahead of all her children. She had been expecting that Marion would want to go off with one of those strange Socialist women she'd been mixing with before she went away, so the alternative was much more acceptable. Marion had proposed that she share some rooms with a girlfriend in Finsbury Park, where she would be much handier for the shop assistant job she had found for herself at Selfridges, the department store in Oxford Street.

"You've got a good head on your shoulders, so there's no reason why you shouldn't be okay with her. Two girls on their own. Weren't like that in my day but that don't mean it's a bad thing." She shrugged in her usual fatalistic way. "Anyway, there aren't many men around in this house these days and we seem to manage okay."

Of Marion's brothers, a pro forma notice dated 1 October 1917 from Infantry Records in Warwick advised Mary that Sergeant T (Tommy) Farrell was wounded whilst serving in Mesopotamia and had been invalided out of the army. Tommy was a bit of a wanderer. Nobody knew what happened to him after 1929, when he was known to be in America. Walter and Bill had left home prior to emigrating; Walter to Australia and Bill to America. All that remained of them were stiff-backed uniformed ghosts on faded sepia photos crowding the mantelpiece in the front room at Barrington Road.

There may have been a more significant reason for Bill's departure to America. He fathered a child, a boy, William, who was born on 19 September 1924 at Alverstone Road, which is just a short walk from Barrington Road. The family thought that Bill may not have been the father but he did marry Amelia a few months before William's birth. The marriage did not work out and Bill left for America after two years, leaving Amelia and William behind. Amelia drowned herself in 1927 and William was brought up by his maternal grandparents. The trail of sadness did not end there. Young William signed up with the army in the Second World War and was killed in 1943 aged nineteen years. Some of this was known within the Farrell family but little was said beyond the fact that Bill had got involved with 'an unstable young woman down the road' and may or may not have been the father of her child. Mary kept his secret until Bill's own daughter in America uncovered it after he died.

Having achieved her goal of leaving home with her mother's approval, Marion was careful to return to Barrington Road every Sunday. However she continued the practice of providing the family with highly sanitised versions of what she got up to. There was no mention of any men in her life and she resisted answering any questions regarding that department. Marion continued to voice alarmingly Socialist views about the war, unions and women's politics. It was a conservative working class household; they knew their place. Her sisters tolerated Marion's eccentric ideas but couldn't really understand why she put so much effort into causes that were outside her control. Her mother would have been equally confused but she seemed to admire her daughter's courage at sticking to her principles however misguided they seemed to others.

In 1921, Marion took a more significant step that was to take her further from the confines of Barrington Road.

2

"I'm fed up with working at Selfridges, Mama," Marion said on one of the Sunday visits to Barrington Road. It wasn't only Selfridges she was fed up with. Even the Labour Party meetings she had begun attending on a regular basis failed to excite her as they once had. All the hand wringing, points of order and petty agenda protocols that dominated meetings of the party seemed to be designed to exclude any real discussion or action. Marion could not be bothered with all the intrigue and point scoring that went on. She'd always liked the idea of nursing but as she was still under twenty-one she would need her mother's approval to apply. And she wasn't sure how she was going to broach the subject.

"Well, I thought you'd go into nursing during the war but you was too young. And, anyway, going off to the Land Army was a good thing to do." Once again her mother was ahead of her, making the rest of the conversation easy.

"It's not that easy getting the nursing qualifications, but I've found out there is a way I could do it," Marion said, forgetting that she was supposed to be undecided about what she was going to do. "If I could get accepted at

15

Colney Hatch as a probationer, I could get qualified as a nurse on the job."

"Colney Hatch? Isn't that the loony bin?" In those days, Colney Hatch was synonymous in the minds of many Londoners with any mental institution. Her mother wasn't so sure that this was such a good idea after all.

"It's a mental hospital. They're not called lunatic asylums any more. But there is proper nursing as well, so I will still get the SRN qualification. And I'd get accommodation with the job. Friern Barnet is in North London. That's not far away and I could come home on my days off." Marion spoke quickly, glossing over the more unappealing aspects of Colney Hatch.

"It's still a loony bin to me, but if that's what you want, you're nearly twenty-one now, old enough to make up your own mind. You'll make a good nurse. Dunno what your sisters are going to make of it."

Marion knew exactly what her sisters would make of it. Still, she had her mother's approval and that was what mattered most. Ironically, by the time the paperwork was completed and she was accepted as a probationer at Colney Hatch, Marion was nearly twenty-two anyway.

The Middlesex County Pauper Lunatic Asylum at Colney Hatch had opened in 1851. Initially it was seen as a symbol of a benevolent state, caring for the more unfortunate in the community. A single-domed tower dominated the approach to the institution. Any sense of peace or haven was dispelled by the impassive functional buildings that sprawled out on either side of the entrance way. Echoing corridors criss-crossed the whole complex and it was quite easy for a newcomer to get lost.

For all the optimistic intent, Colney Hatch soon became a looming Gothic nightmare and a dumping ground for society's misfits. Seventy years after its opening there were two thousand five hundred patients squeezed into buildings designed for nearly half that number. Many had been admitted for serious disorders requiring institutional care, but some ended up there for such conditions as 'intemperance and debauchery', 'fatigue' and 'masturbation'.

It was spring when Marion arrived but it was still winter cold in the building. The flickering gaslights had been lit although it was late afternoon.

Her reception into Colney Hatch is recorded on page 133 of the Female Staff Register:

Marion Farrell. Probationer. Joined 8 May 1922. Pay £1.12.11d per week.

Marion was to live in the nurses' quarters, a short walk from the main building complex. They had been converted from an isolation ward for difficult patients. Nobody had seen the need to remove the bars across the windows.

Marion was an intelligent, pragmatic young woman. If she saw the grim irony of ending up in such a place in her search for an escape from Barrington Road, it was never mentioned.

The induction morals lecture was similar to the one she had received in the Women's Land Army although the delivery of the warning was more direct.

"Men always get away with that sort of thing. I've never seen a male nurse dismissed for impregnating a female, even when they own up to it, which isn't very often. It's the same if you get married. You'd have to leave. Not thinking of getting married are you?" The Sister didn't really expect an answer.

Marion was handed two battered manuals, which were to be the basis of her training, study and part of her qualification.

One, published in 1878 under the auspices of the Commissioners in Lunacy, was titled *Regulations and Orders for the Management of the Asylum for the Pauper Lunatics of the County of Middlesex at Colney Hatch.*[2] This was turgid stuff, full of petty rules devised by some earlier Victorian bureaucracy and couched in challenging language. Instructions about the permitted depth of bath water, the length of tea breaks and punishment for lateness did not hold Marion's interest for long. She thought she would be a good nurse but she could never cope with the cat's cradle of petty rules and hierarchies that locked Colney Hatch into earlier, even more repressive times.

The second manual had been published by the Medico-Psychological

2 *Psychiatry for the Poor* – Hunter, Richard and Macalpine, Ida.

Association in 1885. This was called *Handbook for the Instruction of Attendants of the Insane.* This handbook, with its worn red cover, was much more interesting. There were bland neutered diagrams of the human body and descriptions of basic physiology and how the nervous system worked. Reading it taught Marion what syphilis was and how it affected the brain.

The most humiliating filthy work was saved for the probationers like Marion. With aggressive energy, she scraped at crusted toilet bowls, emptied and washed enamel chamber pots and sorted through soiled bed linen to make sure there were no solid items hidden there before they went down to the laundry. She'd often be called in to scrub the blood from the flagstones after a fight or, sometimes, clear a room after a suicide. All of this, and more, she did quickly, efficiently and without complaint. She would even do darning and mending for the senior staff. Anything to show them she was committed. She was determined to keep her head down, her mouth shut and study for the nursing qualification she had come for.

After some months of this, Sister finally allowed Marion to help with bathing dementia patients. Dementia was a general term covering a wide range of conditions. Some of these patients were in a catatonic state, while others were hyperactive and violent. Patients were bathed once a week. The regulations said that no more than four patients could use the same bath water but a more enlightened regime had since permitted patients to have their own water, provided it was only filled to the mark painted ten inches up the side of the bath.

The female bathroom housed twenty baths for nine hundred patients. The mere process of getting a patient from the ward, into the bath, back out again and dressed ready for bed was a major logistical exercise. Marion had never seen so much naked flesh before. Firm, shrivelled, pendulous, flabby, tall, short, old, young; they were all there. Some of the women were brazen in their nakedness and others lay still in their baths with arms across flattened breasts, hands covering pubic hair. And the noise! Marion was reminded of her Land Army days on the farm and the sound of the pigs squealing in the sty as they chased after swill.

She soon established a reputation for herself as a reliable nurse, popular with the patients. She was occasionally brought in when there was a situation that needed a calm, persuasive voice or just some practical common sense. Her slight build did not seem to be a barrier to her being asked to lift or force-feed patients, prizing open determinedly clamped jaws or pushing thrashing limbs into straitjackets. She was even asked to help the male nurses with some of the more difficult male patients when it was thought that a feminine touch was needed. These special skills were unusual in such a new nurse but Marion was equally at home attending to general nursing situations. She was also in demand to assist the doctors who were usually contemptuous of probationers.

As confidence in her work grew, so did her intolerance of the institutional hierarchy. It was a repressive male-dominated regime designed to ensure that patient 'incidents' were kept to a minimum, often by routinely administered medication. Containment rather than treatment was the priority.

As a probationer, Marion was careful with the other nurses. She listened to the chatter around her, trying to gauge how to gain acceptance in a group where dealing with the abnormal was so normal. It was as if there was no world beyond the institution. Marion laughed hesitantly along with the others at their dark stories. Every bodily function and outrageous situation was subject to merciless examination and laughter. Marion thought at first that this was designed to shock and provoke the newcomers, but it became clear that many of the nurses did not have a life beyond Colney Hatch.

She always remembered one of the nurses talking to her during those first few months. "When I first started, I used to think the nurses were as mad as the patients," the nurse had said. "Sure, a few of them are as potty as the people they lock up, but if you can't laugh at some of the things that happen to you here, you *will* go mad." She had smiled at Marion. "The jokes about blood, shit, vomit and people stringing themselves up are all part of keeping sane. Once it dominates your life, it's time to get out."

By 1925, after three years at Colney Hatch, Marion was a registered nurse, deemed qualified to nurse insane patients. Back at home, her mother was proud of the elaborately scribed nursing certificates that had been delivered to Barrington Road in their important cardboard tubes.

Occasionally, on Marion's visits home, she would talk with her mother after the others had gone to bed. Mostly they talked of family things but sometimes they strayed into difficult areas.

"I'm nursing people who are mad," Marion remembered once saying when she was alone with her mother. "It's not because of anything they've done but because of what's been done to them. As long as they can be locked away out of sight and quietened down with drugs, nobody cares. Some of the poor buggers we have to put in straightjackets think they are still in the trenches and some are locked up just because they are getting on and there is nobody to look after them. I've even had young girls to look after whose only mistake in life is to have caught the pox off the master of the house."

Her mother would not have liked the swearing that was beginning to creep into her daughter's language. She may have also noticed that some of the rough cockney vowels were smoothing out.

Marion was just getting warmed up. "There *are* genuinely mad people there, of course there are. But you can't tell me that all two and a half thousand of them are so nuts they should be banged away in a place like that and given pills and shock treatment to calm them down. From what I've seen, there's a few of the psychiatrists who should be in padded cells anyway."

"They're not interested in changing anything. I think if they looked at what they feed the patients they wouldn't need to use half the medication." This was a theme that Marion frequently returned to since she had started to read up on vegetarianism in *The Healthy Life* magazine. "Some of the menus are straight out of one of those workhouses that Dickens wrote about. I know I've got a chip on my shoulder, Mama. Always will have. But it all seems so bloody unfair."

Her mother flicked at the little strands of snuff that had spilled down the front of her black dress. Vegetarianism, Socialism, it was always best to let Marion run on when she was in this sort of mood. "They're lucky to have you, them people," she said." I think if I had my time again I'd do something like what you're doing." There followed the familiar tight smile and the dismissive shrug of the shoulders to reinforce the inevitability of it all. Marion was sufficiently attuned to take from this that her mother understood why she had decided to leave home. It was even a blessing of sorts.

The rest of the family continued to tolerate their sister's eccentricities. The work with the loonies was cause for much speculation and gossip around the black stove in the back parlour at Barrington Road. Apart from occasionally venting her frustrations to her mother, Marion was careful what she told the rest of the family about the realities and hopelessness of life at Colney Hatch. She was an inventive storyteller. The institution provided a rich storehouse of material from which she would weave dark clever stories to keep her sisters amused. They were never quite sure whether her story of a Jack the Ripper suspect being locked up there was true or not, although her descriptions of creaking doors, jangling keys and the hissing of the inadequate gas lighting were convincing enough. She also hinted darkly that there was a member of the royal family locked up in Colney Hatch.

Marion did not get home as often as she would have liked. Barrington Road was a haven for her after the remorseless, incestuous institutional life at Colney Hatch. Going home, she frequently felt like a prisoner being released from a long sentence. Since she had begun her nursing training, electricity had been connected to Barrington Road and the family huddled around the cat's whisker radio that had replaced the piano as the focal point of their evenings. Marion noticed there were more motor cars and motor buses to be seen around the streets and there was great excitement about the new underground station that was going to be opened at Piccadilly Circus later in 1928. London was changing and she wasn't there to see it.

Her social life was compressed into staff dances and endless gossip about the minutiae of institutional life. She was a qualified nurse with a good record, apart from her tendency to argue with authority. She never forgot the caution about the dangers of becoming as mad as the patients. After six years she was beginning to feel the sticky spider's web of institutionalisation enveloping her.

There is a wide-angled, black and white photograph of all the staff at Colney Hatch taken in May 1928. The professionals, all men, are arranged along the front row. The male nurses are at the back, ties squeezed up into high white collars and jackets tightly buttoned up the front. The female nurses are the only ones in uniform. They are in white with just the headgear to distinguish their place in the nursing hierarchy. Marion is there, smiling her enigmatic smile, the white Sister's cloche hat worn with rakish bravado.

Two months later she was gone. She just walked out.

The Colney Hatch Female Staff Register had columns for dates and reason for leaving. Mostly the reasons given were *to be married*. On 17 August 1928, the registration clerk searched out Nurse Marion Farrell's entry in the register and carefully wrote *'absconded'* against her name as the reason for leaving.

It was as if a patient had escaped; the only difference was that the police weren't notified. Marion's mother was the sole person she told why she left so quickly, and her mother wasn't telling. Her daughter had been quite outspoken about the cruelty of forcible restraints and the introduction of electric shock treatment at Colney Hatch. It may have been some disagreement over treatment at the institution that drove Marion out, although it is just as likely that her volatile temper had got her into trouble. Or perhaps she recognised she was becoming as institutionalised as the patients.

The country was on the brink of the Depression and work was difficult to find, particularly for a young woman who couldn't produce references.

As a subscriber to *Healthy Life Magazine* Marion had developed a regular correspondence with the editor, Edgar Saxon, whilst she had been at Colney Hatch. In addition to the magazine, Saxon was the author of a number of publications advocating a healthy lifestyle, much of it ahead of its time. He also ran an alternative health centre in the West End, which offered alternatives to conventional medicine, including dietary advice, massage and herbal cures. Saxon himself, proudly unqualified, offered lifestyle counselling in person and through correspondence. Many of the clients of the health centre were drawn from the bohemian middle classes.

When Marion came to him for a job, Saxon wasn't worried about her lack of references. She convinced him of her knowledge of alternative medicine and diet. She was attractive and personable and would be an asset to the centre. It would be good to have a qualified nurse on the staff, particularly as Marion had learned therapeutic massage as part of her nursing training at Colney Hatch.

The wages Saxon offered were poor but Marion didn't mind. She was relieved and happy to be working in an environment that was so open to new ways of thinking about medicine and patient care. Some of the clients were quite odd but they all believed in Saxon and were positive about finding alternatives to conventional medicine. Many were captivated by the young nurse with a ready smile and slight cockney accent.

There was an exotic air about Marion at this time. After leaving Colney Hatch she had adopted the name O'Farrell, which was the name Saxon knew her by. The family thought she wanted to identify with her father's long-forgotten Irish ancestors but it was not as complicated as that. She just liked the sound of the name. The 'O' was racier and went with the sandals, long braided hair and flowery dresses she had begun to wear.

She had underestimated how difficult day-to-day living would be outside an institution. It wasn't only money for the board for her digs in Paddington she needed. Travel to work, clothes and food all made inroads into the meagre wages she received from the centre. Although she would always refer to 32 Barrington Road as 'home', she would never return there to live. Saxon offered a few pence per week more but it wasn't enough. She'd have to move on. Within a few weeks of making this decision, she was once more in a nurse's uniform.

An agency sent Marion on private nursing assignments to the houses of the rich around central and west London. It was as if she wanted continually to scratch the itch of class. She didn't mind having to approach houses through the tradesman's entrance or that her nursing qualification, her smart uniform and impressive starched white headgear carried no status in such places. The aged, female, mostly delusional patients saw her as a paid companion/maidservant. Marion was a good listener. She encouraged their confidences and absorbed the insights it gave her to that other world of coming-out parties, champagne breakfasts and finishing schools in Europe. They knew their place as she knew hers. Yet their reliance upon her skills and patience in attending to their sometimes incoherent minds and incontinent bodies brought balance to the relationship. She continued to dabble in alternative medicine, even offering massage to some of her more favoured patients. In the evenings she was able to go off to all sorts of lectures and occasionally attended dances.

On her visits home, she wove a new set of stories to entertain the family. It was always good to have a laugh at the expense of the rich and privileged patients she attended. She remained careful to keep her other life to herself. They knew she went to lectures a lot but she didn't talk much about what went on. Politics had been a sore subject ever since Marion provoked a huge argument at 32 Barrington Road at the time of the 1926 General Strike, when one of the sisters had talked of volunteering to replace striking bus staff. On her visits home, the sisters usually went to the Saturday dance in East Ham. Marion seemed to be up with all the latest dance steps that she had learned in the fancier parts of the city. There was an abandoned and dreamlike quality about her dancing that was enticing but unnerving, even to the boldest of the local young men. Whether there was someone in the city who took her dancing remained a mystery to her sisters. She would soon be thirty, and there was no sign of her bringing a young man home to tea.

3

FAITHFULL, FREEDOM AND
THE WOODCRAFT FOLK

Major Theodore Faithfull has been described by his granddaughter, singer Marianne Faithfull as "the most horrible dirty old man you could imagine".[3] It is not known exactly how Marion met Major Faithfull but she was at that time mixing on the fringes of the bohemian middle classes. Many were parents looking for alternative educational experiences for their children.

Faithfull was one of a small group of educators led by A.S. Neill at Summerhill and including Bertrand Russell at Petersfield, the Elmhirsts at Dartington Hall and George Lyward's Finchden Manor at Tenterden in Kent. They were running schools promoting a freer system of education. Their schools were an antidote to what they saw as the mindless regimentation of conventional schools. Their aim was to create a more democratic school community that treated and respected children as individuals.

Faithfull, late of the Royal Army Veterinary Corps, was the founding Principal and self-styled 'resident psychologist' of Priory Gate School in Norfolk. The prospectus for the school included a photograph of

---

3 *Faithfull* – Faithfull, Marianne with Dolton, David.

Faithfull. He had a handsome, finely chiselled face, with eyes gazing mysteriously into the middle distance. His publications, which were listed in the prospectus, include 'Bisexuality – an essay on extraversion and introversion' and a report of the proceedings of the World Sex Congress, held in London in 1926. He was later to invent a frigidity machine, which he claimed would unblock a woman's primal libido.

Prospective parents were advised of the school's firm commitment to the *Order of Woodcraft Chivalry*. The Order, which had a North American Indian flavour about it, had a gentler, pacifist approach to outdoor education compared to Baden-Powell's more muscular Boy Scout movement. It also differed significantly from the Scouts and Guides in that it did not separate the sexes. Liberal middle-class parents interested in sending their children to Priory Gate were likely to have been familiar with Woodcraft Chivalry. They would not have been fazed by the prospectus that held this description of the school:

Children under eight are known as Elves, from eight to twelve as Woodlings, twelve to fifteen as Trackers and fifteen to eighteen as Pathfinders.

Our children learn at this stage about sociology, self-government and economics by the practical method of coming up against their problems in the school community of which they are now an administrative part, for they have a voice in the making of such rules as may be necessary for the efficient working of the community.

The notion of a school as a community would also have been familiar to those seeking a liberal education for their children.

The prospectus goes on:

They speak without shame of their bodies and natural bodily functions. They also swear when annoyed.

It is part of this natural attitude towards life that we sun battle together on the lawn of the walled garden.

In case the reader is in any doubt about what that meant, the prospectus carries a photograph of some Elves at the river. They are naked.

According to the prospectus, Faithfull believed in the curative effect of nudity on the neurotic child. Naked-culture, in his view, remained one of the chief means that *enables us to get and hold the confidence of the victims of the over-civilisation* of what he called "the Shylock-run world".

Marion seems to have been both attracted and repelled by Major Faithfull and his ideas. Some of the freedoms he was advocating for children made sense to her after the damaging and controlling environment at Colney Hatch and her own experience of the education system. After Colney Hatch, there was nothing that could surprise her, but Faithfull's obsession with sexual behaviour did seem outrageous compared with the more reasoned regimes advocated by A.S. Neill or Bertrand Russell. Marion was tolerant of eccentricity and had a guarded admiration for intellectuals. Faithfull was certainly eccentric and could claim to be intellectual if only for the company he kept.

Viewed through a twenty first century lens, the *Order of Woodcraft Chivalry* outdoor education with its emphasis on 'sun battling' is a strange and possibly dangerous combination for a mixed gender boarding school. Faithfull's apparent obsession with sex and nudity placed him more towards the lunatic edge of the progressive education movement of the time. Yet A.S. Neill at Summerhill and Bertrand Russell at Beacon Hill remained allies of Faithfull, although even the apparently unshockable Neill is on record as being embarrassed by Faithfull on occasion.

Marion enquired about the possibility of work at Priory Gate. Faithfull didn't have any positions available at that stage but would keep her in mind if one turned up. In the meantime he would talk about her with Saxon, whom he knew quite well through the alternative health movement.

In 1930, Faithfull moved his school from Priory Gate to Hazeleigh Lodge in Essex. It is possible that he moved to avoid difficulties and allegations that were beginning to surface around Priory Gate. He had, by then, set himself up as a psychotherapist in London, work that he combined with the principal's role at Hazeleigh. Faithfull offered Marion the job as matron at the new location. It was a grand title that covered a whole range of duties for board and a miniscule salary. She would be responsible for the running of the non-teaching side of the institution, including cooking and cleaning, most of which she carried out herself. The children responded to her dark cockney humour but for more than just the jokes, games and storytelling; the young matron, as the only woman on the small staff, was sought out as a mother figure. She took elementary biology lessons. Entering into the spirit of Faithfull's philosophy, she would occasionally remove her own clothes to illustrate some aspect of female anatomy to a class of ten year olds.

Marion had only been in the job a few weeks when a new young teacher, Morris Horovitch, arrived. Faithfull had an eye for teaching talent and the new man, although not an experienced teacher, had a presence about him that Faithfull must have thought the children would respond to. What he lacked in physical stature, Morris Horovitch made up for with European dark brooding good looks and smiling eyes. Marion, who had an extraordinary ear for London accents, would have easily picked out the Jewish overlay to the barely hidden cockney inflections in his voice. Morris was from Whitechapel, the son of Jewish immigrants. Marion may have wondered how this appointment fitted with Faithfull's apparent anti-Semitism.

Morris liked to talk but he did not take himself too seriously and made no secret about his frustration with his parents' uncompromising Jewish faith. The religion made no sense to him except as a seemingly inexhaustible supply of Jewish jokes. He came from a household where the predominant language was Yiddish. He was as dismissive of his father, Hymie, as Marion was of hers, although Hymie was then still alive. There is no evidence they ever met one another's family.

Morris buckled down to his teaching duties and got on with organising weekend camps and other activities for Elves, Woodlings, Trackers and Pathfinders. Marion kept the institution's home fires burning. They were at ease with one another and tolerant of an environment that challenged the very roots of their own conservative, working-class upbringing.

As well as ingratiating himself with Bertrand Russell and A.S. Neill,

Faithfull maintained links with the Quaker movement and with the more liberal universities, as these were where future parents and, possibly, teachers could be found. University students were encouraged to sample the Hazeleigh experience by joining the weekend camping and hiking programme.

Mary, an attractive and personable young student from the London School of Economics, attended one of these weekends to join a ramble that Morris was organising in the Essex countryside.

She soon became a regular visitor and enthusiastic participant in Morris's rambles. She, too, was escaping a claustrophobic family life. Like Morris and Marion, she was interested in new ideas but she arrived at Hazeleigh from a different starting point. Speech, poise and education marked her clearly as middle class.

Morris was the magnet that drew Mary back each weekend, but she was later careful to describe their friendship at that time as intellectual rather than physical. Marion was then thirty years old, Morris five years younger and Mary, at twenty-one, was the youngest. The three of them, the parties to this strangely shifting triangle, have all since died. Those of us who are left can only speculate on what went on in those years at Faithfull's hothouse at Hazeleigh. Morris, Marion and Mary were to meet again some years later, but by then, their lives would have changed significantly.

Maintaining the financial viability of Hazeleigh was a constant struggle for Faithfull who, according to A.S. Neill, was frequently on the verge of bankruptcy.[4] Marion guessed that the domestic, non-teaching area of the institution would be the first to be affected if Faithfull got into real trouble with money. He had no idea how that side of the institution operated and the costs that were involved. Marion became tired of the constant battle to keep the bills paid, and, after much argument about money, Faithfull dispensed with the services of his matron. The fact that Marion was sacked more as an economy measure than for any concern about her work is reflected in the generous and enthusiastic reference that he gave her. She returned to private nursing.

---

4 *Neill of Summerhill* – Croall, Jonathon.

With Marion gone, Morris found he was more in demand to take groups of children away on hikes for weeks on end. This was a final, inspirational innovation introduced by Faithfull, supposedly to encourage a respect for the outdoors. Morris was not fooled. He had been put in charge of a tented gypsy school that wandered through parts of south-east England, saving Faithfull some of the overhead costs of running the institution.

Mary accompanied Morris on some of these trips but finally decided against visiting Hazeleigh any more. She later said she did not want her friendship with Morris to get too serious.

Inevitably Faithfull's experiment in progressive education foundered. He closed the school and decided to concentrate on his psychotherapy practice in London, which was at least paying the bills. So in 1932, just a few months after Marion had been sacked, Morris also found himself looking for work as Faithfull moved to close his school. Morris and Marion had been together at Hazeleigh for just over a year.

Private nursing provided an income but Marion found it frustrating and lonely work. Her time with Faithfull had shown that she could cope in that sort of environment; it was now just a matter of finding somewhere that had a more stable financial base than Faithfull had offered at Hazeleigh.

4

OTTO SHAW AND
RED HILL SCHOOL

It was a freezing dark Sunday afternoon in January 1934 when Marion crossed the river to south London to meet Otto Shaw for the first time.

Shaw was a large young man, bulging with complexities, contradictions and intelligence. At twenty-seven, he was said to have a doctorate in chemistry and had apparently been destined for a successful career as an industrial chemist with Shell. Why he would want to give all that away in order to set up a private school for maladjusted children has never been clear, but there are many who are glad he did and one or two who wish they had never crossed his path.

In 1934, Shaw was looking for teachers and a nursing-housekeeper for his new school to be located at Red Hill in Chislehurst, where suburban London reaches into Kent. Shaw was an admirer of A.S. Neill's work at Summerhill and he was determined to find staff capable of managing without the disciplines and hierarchies of conventional boarding schools. Like Neill, Shaw was condescending about Faithfull, but he guessed that anyone who could manage in the Hazeleigh environment should be able to cope with what he had in mind for his new school.

There was still an air of the bohemian about Marion but she knew enough to dress conservatively for an interview with a prospective employer. The house in New Eltham where Shaw was living with his mother was like so many where Marion had passed through the tradesman's entrance in her days of private nursing. She thought she knew what to expect when the large figure opened the door to her and briefly introduced her to his mother. In many ways, Shaw would have fitted comfortably into Marion's view of the stereotype of the middle-class academic with whom she had become so familiar. Shaw had been educated at a minor south London public school, Eltham College. He was arrogantly confident of his place in the world, but like many other ex-public schoolboys, he had retained some of the naivety and unease around women. Marion was unprepared for the overwhelming charm and the sharp humour of the man as he talked of socialism, the shortcomings of the conventional educational system and his vision for Red Hill School.

Shaw was vehemently opposed to corporal punishment. He claimed beatings would have no part in the regime of the new school. He envisaged creating an environment where the children would, for the most part, make the rules and deal with misbehaviour in the school community. Like Faithfull, he used the term 'psychotherapy' rather loosely and his professional qualifications to provide this service were as questionable as Faithfull's. He was a Freudian, but he had his own distinctive views.

There would be a mix of both sexes and Shaw expected the ages to range from the quite young through to late adolescence. A.S. Neill and others had done a lot of the groundwork and showed that progressive schools could be a viable alternative to more traditional approaches to education, but the first year or two was going to be hard. Shaw felt he could develop some influence in local politics so was aiming to get referrals from educational authorities, but there would also be reliance upon private fee-paying children. He had obviously thought through some of the practicalities of balancing the books. Fees apart, admission to Red Hill would be determined by the intelligence level of the child and the child's ability to cope with the freer regime. Shaw was confident his school could manage the most difficult, disturbed and often highly gifted children.

Marion's job would be central to the running of the school but it would require patience and skill. Shaw did not expect there to be any other women on the staff, although he was planning a role for his mother. Marion was able to pick up much about his background from the way he spoke. Middle-class south London, minor public school she guessed, correctly. He peppered his conversation with graphic swear words but whether that was to ingratiate himself, intimidate her or just the thrill of shocking an attractive woman, she was not sure. She had travelled a long way from Barrington Road by then and there was not much that could shock her.

She had inherited her mother's dismissive, philosophical shrug. She needed to show that she knew what she was talking about, that she was experienced in the ways of institutions; certainly more experienced than him.

Shaw continued for another half an hour, baiting his conversation with provocative assertions that he drew in front of her like a lure. She had met cleverness before and was not unsettled by his approach. She watched his thin lips smile in ironic approval of her embellished accounts of life at Colney Hatch, the stories the family at Barrington Road had so enjoyed. Her account of Hazeleigh was full of black cynical observations but she obviously had a soft spot for the place and some admiration for Faithfull.

"I think you should join us then," Shaw said, leaning back, with his hands behind his head, spotted bow tie wobbling against his thick neck. "I'll need you at the school all the time, so you'll have to live in. I'll arrange for you to have a room there." He was aware of his physical presence and ability to dominate a room, even when he was sitting. He used it sparingly but when he did, he was an overwhelming force that few would choose to challenge.

Now they were at the business end of the discussion, Shaw became brisk and dismissive. The salary was appalling by any standards and was reduced further by the rent for the room in the school that went with the job. Marion was able to negotiate a half day off per week along with some small concessions around Christmas and summer holidays. Many of the children would have no homes to go to. The school would never close and her presence, day and night, was a given. For all his socialist principles, Shaw exploited some of his staff. It was something Marion would continually remind him of over the next thirty years. He was implacable when she tentatively challenged the salary being offered. His extraordinary generosity of spirit did not extend to money and there was a lot of his own money tied up in the school. She agreed to start the next month. She was thirty-four and had her mentor and leader. He had crossed his social divide and discovered an unlikely confidante and a cornerstone for his venture. It was to be an uneasy, unbalanced alliance, given Shaw's secretive complex nature and his ability to control and manipulate.

The residents of the south London suburb of Red Hill in Chislehurst would have viewed with some alarm the arrival of the first three or four pupils at what was to be called Red Hill School. It was 1934. Tony Watson, at six, was the youngest. He remembers himself as a young working class tearaway, quite out of the control of his parents and the welfare agencies assigned to his care. Another boy in that first group but from a completely different background from Tony was David Baden-Powell, from the Scouting family. Tony, David and the others struggled to work out what was required of them when it appeared that there were no rules at Red Hill worth breaking.

As far as the residents of Chislehurst were concerned, anarchy ruled. With the roll increasing to ten or so, there were soon rumours of smoking, swearing and, with ill-disciplined girls and boys together, well, who knew what they got up to? The new neighbour was a threat in so many ways, to say nothing of property values. Shaw thought the attitude of the residents was unfair but he was unsuccessful in his efforts to win them over. He realised he would never achieve his vision of a school community in such a hostile suburban environment and, after a few months, was looking for a more suitable location.

He finally found Charlton Court, overlooking the Weald of Kent in East Sutton, near Maidstone. Built for Sir Edward Filmer in the seventeenth century, Charlton Court had housed the Filmer-Wilson family for about two hundred years. In 1915 the building was commandeered as a military hospital and was later converted by the Caldecott Community for use as a boarding school for working men's children. With its high red-brick Tudor chimneys, walled garden, sweeping driveway and dark oak staircases, Charlton Court had seen off all its invaders and was ready to re-establish itself as a dignified country manor house. Shaw had other plans. A lease was signed with the owners, and in 1935, Charlton Court became Red Hill School.

A board was appointed but Shaw was the only person in the place who had a clear vision for Red Hill and how it would all work. Furthermore he had no experience at all of running an educational institution beyond what he had learned from voracious reading on the subject and occasional visits to A.S. Neill at Summerhill. As at Summerhill, establishing a democratic community within the school was to be key to the whole Red Hill approach.

Shaw carefully recruited the five or so people upon whom the success of Red Hill would depend. Early staff meetings in the smoke-filled room at the bottom of the backstairs were notable more for arguments than for any cohesive approach to running a school. There was intellect and ego to burn amongst those early staff members, but there was very little experience of running a school, let alone a school community based on such free educational concepts. Shaw calmly presided over the initial chaos that followed as the children, most of whom had some previous experience in pushing the boundaries of conformity, tested the environment around them.

Marion was initially overwhelmed by the bewildering array of accents, backgrounds and intellects that competed for attention in the tiny staff room. Hazeleigh and Colney Hatch had prepared her well for such pyrotechnics, however. Words would soon crash and burn and then they would be looking for some practical solutions. That was when she would come in. There was a core group of salaried staff supplemented by an array of temporary teachers, embryonic psychologists and the odd drifter who had been able to convince Shaw he had something to offer.

Marion's role quickly expanded. She was not interested in educational theory but saw some of what Shaw wanted at a practical level and she provided the common sense and determination to get things working. If that meant doing the cooking when the cook didn't turn up or taking a junior nature study class then that's what she did, although she was often heard to complain bitterly about being exploited. She also introduced some of the milder practices of the Woodcraft folk she and Morris had experienced at Hazeleigh.

Shaw grafted on to Red Hill many of the standards and practices of his own public school experience. There were to be no houses or uniforms, but Red Hill had a glossary of public school terminology that the inventive community of children bent to their own experience and vocabulary. From this, a unique Red Hill tradition would be fashioned.

Gradually, the notion of a school community did take hold, and some ground rules and standards were established through regular community meetings. Small sub-committees of children were elected to oversee such activities as food and hygiene, building maintenance, and social and sporting activities. It wasn't much different from the local borough council in Maidstone. There was still a determination not to use any form of physical coercion to enforce the rules and standards that were being set.

Shaw provided the professional leadership and worked individually with children. "I'm going to Shaw for Freudian analysis" was soon an established and acceptable reason to be absent from the classroom. Initially, the teaching component of the school was secondary to the development of the school community itself. Although Red Hill was never known for conventional educational results, many ex-pupils did go on to high academic achievement.

With these preliminary structures in place, the school community grew in confidence. There were sometimes frustrations within the community that very occasionally erupted into violence between the pupils, but soon systems for resolving disputes were found and used. Shaw always maintained that he never resorted to corporal punishment, but there were exceptions. I have since spoken to two boys who complained that they were quite savagely beaten by Shaw in those early days at Red Hill.

Marion's increasing sense of her value to the school led to an outspokenness that would eventually land her in trouble with some of those on the staff whom she regarded as not contributing. A particular target for her vitriol was Lily, the wife of the Deputy Principal, Ivor Holland. Lily, through Marion's eyes anyway, was keen to claim for herself early on whatever status went with her husband's role. Factions quickly formed around the two women with Shaw identifying Marion, much to her indignation, as the troublemaker. She resigned. Shaw called her bluff and provided a glowing reference. The resignation was never withdrawn but neither did it go ahead. A battle of wills had, for the time being, ended in an honourable draw.

As the roll grew, many of the children looked immediately to Marion as the mother they had not known. To some of the teenage girls, she was less mother and more elder sister although she was by then approaching forty years old. She was someone to share a smoke and a gossip with in the dark cosy room that she had been allocated above the kitchen in the main building. The nine o'clock news on Marion's crackly old valve wireless was the centrepiece for many Red Hill evenings at that time. Younger children turning up for their bedtime stories would sometimes find themselves caught up in furious debates on the rights and wrongs of the abdication of the Prince of Wales on 10 December 1936 or Winston Churchill's warnings about German rearmament. Some would join in and some would just fall asleep in her lap before getting carted off to their dormitory, bedtime stories postponed until another night when the news was less provocative.

She seemed to have an easier relationship with the children than she did with some of her colleagues. Male colleagues were all aware that the self-deprecating cockney humour and delicate, attractive face should not be taken for weakness. She threw herself into the school's social life, helping to organise dances, concerts, and rambles through the rolling Kent countryside. At the dances she was the uninhibited one, unplaited hair flowing and animated face thrown back in laughter, dancing to the sound of bands like Jimmy Shand or Joe Loss creaking out on the wind-up gramophone. She knew all the steps and would never say "no" to a dance, whether the prospective partner be adult or child. If needed, she'd play the piano, bashing out *The Lambeth Walk* and some of the old music hall numbers she'd learned from visits to the Palace at East Ham. It was difficult to separate this warm, vivacious woman who was so much at the centre of things from the waspish, foul-mouthed harridan that could be unleashed if she felt she was being slighted or that her patch needed defending.

The First World War had ended only twenty years previously and already there was talk of another war with Germany. It was the time of appeasement and little was heard in England about the persecution of Jews in Germany. Not that many would have cared. As Marion well knew from Faithfull and from growing up in the East End, many in the English establishment and the working class also saw Jews as outsiders. Oswald Mosley and the Fascists who had marched through East Ham were just the tip of the iceberg. It was against this particular tide in his own country that Shaw was rumoured to have taken trips to Germany to see what he could do to bring out refugees from under the noses of the Nazis. The school buzzed with speculation that he was posing as a salesman in order to make his contacts. Soon, one or two names like Mueller and Steinberg began to appear on the school roll, joining the growing number of, mostly boys, referred by local authorities as being too difficult to handle in conventional education environments.

Marion wasn't always able to hide her contempt for what she saw, sometimes incorrectly, as intellectual and social privilege amongst the staff at Red Hill. She found herself drawn to the more outrageous and rebellious faction within a highly opinionated and individualistic group. She had the fearlessness of a shop steward as far as her own area was concerned, and teaching staff knew to be wary around her.

Len Bloom is one man who had a long history with Red Hill School, both as a boy in the 1930s and then as a staff member, before embarking upon a highly successful career as a child psychologist. He has described Marion in those earlier years as a Beatrice Lillie lookalike. Bea Lillie was a well-known actress of the time. It has been said that Lillie's great talents were the arched eyebrows, the curled lip, the fluttering eyelid, the tilted chin and the ability to suggest, even in apparently innocent material, the possible double entendre. Marion would have been pleased and flattered by the comparison. She certainly had that presence about her. Len remembered the risqué jokes and the music hall Irish accent she affected when she read James Stephens' novel *The Crock of Gold* to him and some of the other children before bedtime. Her little room had become a focal point for bedtime stories for the smaller children or a smoke and chat for some of the older ones, particularly the teenage girls.

Marion was still using the name Marion O'Farrell and this soon was abbreviated in the manner of schoolchildren. For the rest of her life at Red Hill she was to be known by staff and children alike as MOF. She was lucky. Shaw's deputy, Ivor Holland, the cerebral self-reflective counterpoint to Shaw's overwhelming presence, was forever and for obvious reasons destined to be Baldy.

The members of permanent staff listed as employed around the outbreak of war in 1939 show Holland as educational director, his wife Lily as kindergarten teacher, and a Miss J. Fletcher, as teacher. In addition there was a gardener, Ted Brown, who had previously been employed at Charlton Court. Miss M. O'Farrell is shown under Nursing Staff.

The other member of the permanent teaching staff is listed as Mr M. Horovitch (Board of Education Teaching Certificate). This is the same Morris Horovitch who worked with Marion at Hazeleigh Lodge. It seems likely that Morris was at Red Hill School for about two years from 1938, although there is no other record of him being there; neither can any surviving pupil recall his presence. It is difficult to see Shaw's recruitment of Morris as a coincidence and it is safe to assume that Morris and Marion were pleased to recommence the friendship that had begun at Hazeleigh. Mary, the young student Morris had met at Hazeleigh, had apparently ended her relationship with him.

5

HARSH REALITIES

That Marion and Morris became lovers is indisputable. The only information about the length and depth of the affair, and what it meant to her, appears in the poetry she wrote at the time. She was dismissive of and embarrassed by her writing, but she took care to ensure her poems were in her papers to be found many years later. Although I'd like to think that I was conceived from a union of mutual love, her writing indicates that this was probably not the case.

Marion's eldest sister Agnes and her mother found reading and writing quite difficult and they struggled to make sense of Marion's letters from that strange school where she worked. Anyway, Marion was careful not to give them any lines to read between.

She loved the sound of words and used them with pitiless honesty when she wrote about herself. The poems all untitled, mostly unpunctuated and written in a strong sloping hand, provide some record of the most tumultuous time of her life. This poem hints at the rawness and vulnerability she was then feeling.

A whisper comes in the lonely night
Causing my heart to flinch

My body becomes a fire
Which burns and tortures me
And, like molten lava,
Gushing from the womb of the mountain,
Runs in a hot steaming stream, finding its own level
So, the liquid fire of me, the essential essence of me,
Stretches forth blind hands, searching for thee
Morning comes, the darkness passes
Stilled is my heart, with silence
My soul struggles above desire
Like a phoenix rising
From the ashes of a dead fire
Comes the whisper of thy voice
Rippling like golden threads, weaving through the wool
The gloom of my unquiet spirit, and the central core of me
Responds to the call of thee,
Raising suppliant hands, pleading to thee.

In a later precursory moment, she talks of her lover giving her:

More than I dreamed of
If less than you vowed

During July 1939 she must have missed her period. She may have felt a slight shiver of anxiety, but after all she was forty. She knew what the vagaries of middle age could do to a woman's body. She wasn't too worried. She'd wait and see what happened next month.

Meanwhile, the debates in her little room were taking a dangerous turn. The outside world was beginning to impinge upon life at Red Hill in a significant way. All through the morning of 3 September 1939, the Home Service interrupted bland music with warnings of a coming announcement, presumably from the King. However, it was the reedy-voiced Prime Minister, Neville Chamberlain, who made the formal declaration of war against Germany. Then the King, his stutter barely discernible, made his call to arms with warnings of dark days ahead.

Both men put their trust in God. Marion wasn't sure that God was going to be much help, but she was a royalist and excluded the royal family from the class war. She trusted the King; Churchill was a different matter. She felt he represented all that was wrong with a system that gave those of high birth the right to rule. However, she did grudgingly accept that Churchill might make a good wartime leader, now it had come to that. Later news bulletins that day advised listeners to keep off the streets and carry gas masks at all times and, ominously, sew labels with names and addresses into children's clothing so they couldn't be torn off.

A widely expected German invasion based on the coast around Kent placed Red Hill squarely in the path of any occupying army on its way to London. The authorities were making discreet plans to commandeer Charlton Court as a hospital once more as they had in the first war. There was a plan to evacuate Red Hill School to Worcester. The one or two refugees within the small school community had most reason to be fearful; they had some inkling of what life might be like under an occupying force.

Marion knew she was pregnant. She needed to talk with Morris. He was five years younger than her and still bursting with ambition. The only thing she was sure of was that she would have the child and bring it up herself, if that was what it took. She appeared to have no idea whether or not Morris would stay with her, and she may well have had reservations of her own about sharing her life with someone else. That first conversation must have been painful for them both. They decided to talk with Shaw. He had far less experience of life and the practicalities of human relationships than either of them, but Shaw would know what to do.

Like disturbed children going for analysis, they went to see Shaw in his study. It's unclear whether Shaw had anything to do with their decisions to part and for Morris, rather than Marion, to leave the school. Marion felt humiliated for herself, angry at Morris, and anxious for the unborn child. Shaw offered to see her through this, keeping her on staff and providing her with a larger room so she could share it with the baby when it was born. For Marion, accepting Shaw's generosity entailed involving him in all her significant subsequent life decisions from then on. It seemed a small price to pay for the security offered.

Shaw arranged a quiet departure for Morris and recommended him for placement at a school in Hertfordshire. Morris would miss Red Hill and was determined to keep in touch with Shaw, whom he admired tremendously. In his role of mentor and adviser to Morris and to Marion, Shaw also became a go-between, managing the communication between them. Shaw ensured that the nature of their relationship was kept secret, even from the son yet to be born.

Around this time, Marion wrote:

I don't know why it hurt me so
Or why I should have cared
Because a man was motley clad
Chalk faced and saffron haired
And yet he haunted me for days
And once or twice I cried
For when his eyes looked into mine
I saw all hope had died

By Christmas 1939, things were strangely quiet in Kent. Men were still departing for Europe much as they had for the earlier war, but there was an ominous, tense peace. In the little linen room at Red Hill, so small it was called 'the linen cupboard', MOF complied with the bidding of the Home Service and began stitching name and address labels into the pupils' clothing. There was still no sign of jackboots crunching down the front drive, but the school community found it had other things to think about.

MOF was pregnant and, by the look of her, the baby was due in four or five months. She had taken to wearing a wedding ring, although no one had heard of any wedding. There was no father in evidence. Those at Red Hill thought to be in the know favoured Shaw for the role. The fact that he had recently married only added spice to the rumours. The rumours were wrong but nobody seemed to connect her pregnancy with the departure of Morris Horovitch. Marion later wrote:

I know my body was unfaithful
But did my body count so much
Beside the many other things
My love builded for you
That all the whispering mouths of our desire and sympathy
Should be struck dumb
I feel so helpless in the face of this
So stricken, while my heart
Still holds the transcendental
Wonder of my worship
Holds it fast, seething
Like a heavy harnessed tide
That only your compassion can release
You are yet young
And I, I am not old
Let us leave this barren rock
And put to sea. The waves will bear us up again to joy
While death stays cheated
On the shore

MOF's pregnancy didn't seem to make any difference to her relationships with the children, but she continued to attract unswerving loyalty and enmity in equal measure from her colleagues. Some noticed that her ironic wit had taken a cynical edge. Men, particularly, learned to be even more wary around her. Ruth, one of the domestic staff, seems to have been her only confidante; it was Ruth to whom she poured out her fears about how her family at Barrington Road was going to take the news. It was Ruth who listened when she agonised about bringing a child into the world with invasion forces just a few miles away across the Channel.

I shall forget you
Yet, I dread the hour when you'll no longer fill my secret dreams

And thoughts, my tender prayers.
Though some greater love, all unawares, will claim me,
I shall miss the joyous thrill, that heralded your nearness
And yet, your smile, your eyes, all that I prize
I shall forget.

She grew increasingly anxious about her mother and family's reaction to her pregnancy, remembering the awful silence that blanketed discussion about her brother Bill's transgression before he left for America. Nobody knew what had happened to that child, or if they did they weren't saying. She was torn. There was the bleak prospect of being an unmarried mother to a child with a Jewish father in an increasingly dangerous world; there was the bitterness of lost love. She considered hiding the news from her mother, but she knew that was one secret she would not be able to keep from her.

In any case, where could she have this baby? The hospital in Maidstone would not take a perfectly healthy mother-to-be, however old she was. Didn't she know there was a war on? Having the baby at Red Hill was out of the question, although she knew the village doctor from nearby Sutton Valence would come out for her. Apart from Ruth, she didn't know of anyone else she could call upon. And for all her toughness, she didn't want to become a source of embarrassment with the children at Red Hill. As her body began to swell, so their curiosity grew. There were the questions from the children, direct and matter-of-fact.

"Where will it come out of when it's born?"

"How did it get in there? Did you have to fuck someone?"

"Will it be a bastard, MOF?"

There was little that was sacred. She was part of the Red Hill regime that encouraged open questioning of everything, so she could hardly complain now that same curiosity was directed towards her. She became very skilled at fending it off with nonsensical responses.

By December 1939, Marion's sister Hilda and her husband Cecil had evacuated from Ilford to Bletchley in Buckinghamshire with their daughter Sheila, then aged five. Hilda had no idea that Marion was pregnant when she issued the invitation to her sister to visit them all at Bletchley, where they would be safe from any bombing. Marion had by that time accepted Shaw's offer to remain at Red Hill with the child. She had put off telling her mother and was still uneasy about the likely reception at Barrington Road. Her reply to Hilda was guarded:

Thank you so much for your letter but in view of the fact I shall be having a long holiday early in the New Year, I think it would be better to wait.

She had continued to keep to herself what was going on in her own social life. She lived her life in compartments and nobody had the keys to the interlocking doors. There was the dutiful daughter and sister who visited Barrington Road; there was Red Hill; there were friends; there was, or had been, Morris. Soon there was to be another compartment marked 'mother'.

She needed to stop being MOF for a while. She needed her family. Facing her mother was going to take all of her remaining reserves of strength.

Mary Farrell (Grandma), the matriarch of the Farrell family. She had 13 children.

Poster for the Women's Land Army.
Photo: Getty Images.

Barrington Road, Manor Park, East Ham, London, as it looks today.

Agnes, Grandma and Marion, 1930s.

Women working in a munitions factory in the First World War. *Photo: Getty Images.*

Colney Hatch opened as the Middlesex
County Pauper Lunatic Asylum in 1851.
Marion worked there from 1922–1928.
Photo: English Heritage.

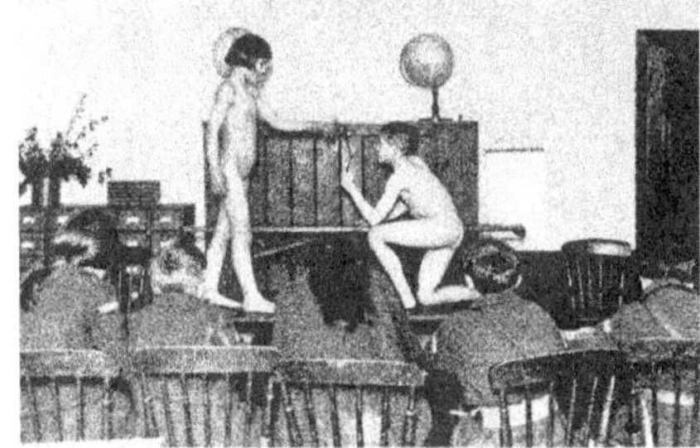

This is taken from the school prospectus for
Priory Gate School, which Major Faithfull ran
before opening Hazeleigh.

Marion was sent on various private nursing
assignments once she left Colney Hatch.

Major Theodore Faithfull. Marion worked
for him at his progressive school in Hazeleigh
where she first met Morris Horovitch.

Red Hill School in Kent, my home for 17 years.

Marion and staff at Red Hill, probably 1941.

Otto Shaw, the founding principal of Red Hill School. A complex, charismatic man of many talents who led Red Hill for 40 years.

Shaw stood for Labour in the safe Tory seats of Maidstone (in 1945 and 1957) and Thanet (in 1951).

Marion at around the time she met Morris for the first time at Hazeleigh.

Marion in the late 1930s.

Marion in the 1930s.

PART 2
PETER

6

THE LIE

By the time Marion made her way up to London to see her mother the air raid sirens were still screeching their false alarms across the East End. Anxious faces peered up into the empty sky. Yet still the bombers did not come. Once Marion decided what she was going to do, she set about preparing her mother for the news. She could not just turn up at Barrington Road, eight months pregnant. That would be too much, even for her mother. So, for the first time, her mother received a letter from her daughter that contained real news rather than the usual stuff about the war and the weather in Kent. There was no mention of who the father of the child might be. Her mother speculated whether it was this Shaw that Marion had gone on about, as if he were some sort of expert on everything.

On the front steps of 32 Barrington Road, they looked at one another. The old lady, dressed in her comfortable, long black dress looked so assured and so wise. The younger woman in front of her had aged; the bright eager face had sagged a little and was lined with bitterness. Marion bent awkwardly as she gently placed her suitcase in the tiny hallway. Mother and daughter touched gingerly, as if concerned they would hurt each other. Marion's sister Agnes hovered in the hall. As the eldest, it would be Agnes's job to see their mother through the last stage of life. Agnes and her husband George, along with the old lady, were all that were left of the family living at Barrington Road.

"You're home now. If there's one thing we know about in this house, it's having kids." Old Mary smiled a rare, toothy smile as she bustled around the suitcase. "I've put you in that little box room upstairs. It won't be the first baby born up there, I can tell you. Get yourself sorted and I'll bring up a cuppa tea. Then you can tell me what's been going on."

"No mama, it isn't Shaw," Marion said, in answer to the question she had known was coming. "It's someone else on the staff at Red Hill, a teacher. I've known him a long time." There was no room for a chair in the room so they had settled down on the bed, drinking their tea and picking at a piece of Agnes's fruitcake her mother had brought up from downstairs. The bed squeaked as her mother shifted her body to face Marion, while avoiding looking directly at her.

"What's his name then, this teacher?" She did not have Marion's reservations about the professions. She respected education and what it could do for you.

"Morris Horovitch," Marion said with a tight bitter smile.

"Foreigner is he? Jew, by the sound of it." She wasn't judging anything, but she did need to know.

"His parents are Jews. Came here from Austria or somewhere but he was born up Whitechapel way. He's more cockney than us," she added, by way of reassurance.

Her mother was incredibly curious about this man, but she also knew Marion well enough not to ask where he was now and why he had scarpered. She may or may not get the whole story someday, but there was still something else about the situation that needed sorting out for the family's sake.

"What are we going to tell Agnes and the others? I know she's taken up with the Salvation Army since she married George but she's not going to believe in no virgin birth! And there is also the little one to think about.

What are you going to tell him about his dad?" Mary always assumed her own children would be boys, so there was no reason why it would be any different with this grandchild. She was more comfortable now that they were moving to the safer, practical territory where she excelled.

"I don't know, Mama. I have to protect the baby. That's all I can think about. I'm going to keep my own name and just tell people that I changed it back after my husband got killed in the war. It's common enough nowadays." She was inviting her mother to be party to the lie and to promote it within the family. Marion would need Shaw's help to promote the story at Red Hill. How Morris dealt with it was up to him.

"No love. We can't do that." Her mother was going to help. "What you tell the little one is your business, but our girls are never going to believe that you got married, got pregnant and became a widow all in the space of nine months or so and you didn't tell them a thing." The bed in the box room protested again as she shifted her body into a more comfortable position, waiting for Marion's response.

"You're right, Mama. They wouldn't believe that, even of me!" She knew what they thought of her and her lifestyle. "But I don't think I can face them. Can *you* tell them? I know you've done it once before." The older woman lowered her eyes and nodded. It was likely that Bill's boy, William, was still living a few minutes' walk away at Alverstone Road.

"We'll just have to trust them to keep it from the boy as he grows up," Marion continued more to herself, making the same assumption as her mother about the gender of her child. "God knows there will be enough for him to cope with without knowing I'm not married and his father has scarpered. As far as the boy is concerned, his dad died in the war."

So they agreed that her mother would tell the family as much as she knew, and they would rely upon the Farrell family conspiracy of silence to protect its newest member from the truth.

A month later, on 23 April 1940, the baby was born in the box room upstairs at number 32. All the sisters were there; they didn't need a midwife. There wasn't much you could tell the old lady about the process of giving birth. Grace's daughter Jo was playing in the front room. She heard the commotion coming from upstairs. Grace came down and told Jo she had a new cousin. A boy.

"Where's his dad?" she asked her mother. A reasonable question for a ten year old particularly as Auntie Marion was a favourite of hers. A free spirit. Grace was evasive and Jo knew immediately she would not get an answer to her question. It was not a question she would ever ask again. "What's his name then?" Jo asked.

"I think she's going to call him Peter."

In the month that followed my birth, Marion received a reassuring telegram and letter from Ruth, who was keen to keep her up to date with what she called the backstairs gossip at Red Hill. There was also a letter from Shaw. Apparently Morris had visited Red Hill but Shaw was not forthcoming about the purpose of the visit. Shaw advised her to write to Morris at a place called Bunce Court, where he was then working. Shaw's letter finished warmly:

When are you coming for a weekend at the bungalow? Try and make it soon, as there are many things I want to talk over with you. If you cannot leave Peter (is that his name?), bring him with you.

Don't worry about the future; surely there will be some way to sort it out.

A few weeks later, she went down to Kent to see Shaw and his wife Joan at the bungalow on Chart Road on the outskirts of Sutton Valence. Joan Goodbody was beautiful, sophisticated and well established on the Maidstone social scene. There was some surprise when she agreed to marry the gauche yet brilliant principal of Red Hill who was already beginning to make his presence felt in local politics as an unlikely advocate for socialism. Marion and Joan developed an odd, distant friendship. Shaw had introduced them in the hope they would get on. He may have reasoned that Marion, in her practical way, would help Joan understand what Red Hill was all about. Joan would later attend school events as part of her role as the dutiful wife to an unpredictable, charismatic husband with political ambitions. Red Hill boys often visited Shaw's house in the village. But mostly Joan was a remote figure at the school.

Joan was herself heavily pregnant at the time of Marion's visit. Shaw was excluded from much of the conversation as the two women exchanged stories of motherhood. Shaw, always uncomfortable with domesticity, fidgeted in his chair until Marion said it was time for her to go. She needed to get the baby back to London before the blackout.

"I'll take you to Maidstone to catch the train. We can talk in the car," he said, reaching for the keys to his Wolseley.

Shaw was the only person Marion knew who had a car. He was a good driver even if he did like to go too fast. She was happy to agree, although she was apprehensive about what he wanted to talk about that he couldn't say in front of Joan.

"I've told Morris about Peter and that you're both okay." Shaw knew the road well so was able to look across at Marion without reducing speed. "He told me he is quite settled himself – met a woman called Mary someone or other. Said you might know her."

Mary, the one from the London School of Economics, the one who visited at Hazeleigh. Marion's mouth tightened, but she said nothing.

They got to the station in plenty of time but she hung around, waiting for the London train. There were chalkboard notices referring to delays, which could only have meant something to do with the war. She wondered whether the bombing had started and what she might find at Barrington Road. When she eventually got to London, the platforms at Victoria were crowded with soldiers arriving back from France. She held her baby more tightly to her and made her way to the Underground and the safe familiarity of the District line. It was not far to walk to Barrington Road from East Ham Station.

The visit to Shaw's bungalow at Sutton Valence had been amicable enough and she was looking forward to getting back to Red Hill. In the car, he had also talked about the possibility of Red Hill vacating Charlton Court and moving to a safer location in Worcester. She didn't mind going there, as that would make it easier to make a new start as a respectable widow.

A few days after her return to Barrington Road, Shaw sent out a typed letter that was circulated to all the staff. In it, he said he had been concerned about damaging divisions growing in the staff room, particularly with the possibility of the school being evacuated to Worcester. He was insistent that he was looking for an improvement from them all. In an addendum to Marion's own copy, he reassured her that the letter was not directed at her personally, but then he went on to write:

Please be very guarded in your attitude towards those here, including myself with whom your past relations have not been too good. You are unlikely to encounter any bad feelings from others, but you could create bad feelings by tactless or premature advances or by creating factions. The latter must not happen.

All regards and love to Peter.
Shaw.

A year previously she would have bridled at the suggestion, implicit in his words, that she was the cause of the divisions within the staff. However things were different now and she would do nothing to put the future of her son at risk. There would be no question of reactivating that earlier resignation. She would have to see the storm out. She was no longer in a position where she could just move on.

Her sisters had been loving and discreet about her situation, although she knew she would be the subject of gossip whenever they got together on their own. She was surprised at how easily she fitted into the role of mother and how much she enjoyed the baby's dependency upon her. She had never felt so close to her own mother as she did during those few weeks after the baby was born. The old lady expressed herself powerfully, but in undertones. It might be a grim smile or a throwaway joke, but you always knew what she meant. She was not demonstrative in her gestures and struggled to speak about emotional things. It would be very tempting to stay in the comfortable environment at Barrington Road, bombing or no bombing, but Marion belonged at Red Hill with Shaw, the tensions and the kids. There was one last thing she had to tell her mother. They were sitting in the front room, waiting for Agnes's husband George to bring in the tin bath. It was the usual routine. They'd bathe the baby first. Then one of the adults, whoever was due for a bath, would wait for the others to leave, before topping up the tepid, soapy water from the bucket of boiling water on the stove.

"Shaw told me something when I was down there the other week." She struggled to keep her voice level. "He said Morris has gone back to one of his other women friends. It's the one called Mary. We both knew her at Hazeleigh, years ago. She was more Morris's friend than mine. I didn't like her much, just swanning in from the university at the weekends, visiting. Playing at it really."

Marion paused, remembering the poised capable young woman with the imposing accent that, for some reason, made her think of tennis clubs and cocktails on the lawn, although Marion had no experience of either. "She's a lot younger than me. Pretty, too. And Morris was always impressed by intellect. Shaw hinted that wedding bells may not be too far away."

Her mother raised a fierce eyebrow. "Didn't take him long, did it?" she said emphatically and then shrugged.

"Still, it's his loss. You're well out of it, love. Come on, let's get this boy ready for his bath. He's a lucky little nipper to have you. You're not going to let nobody down, least of all him." She grunted as she lowered the baby into the warm soapy water of the tin bath.

A week later, back in her little room at Red Hill with the baby in the cot beside her, Marion allowed herself one more indulgent black thought.

I sit in a daze, and count the years wasted
Years that could have been so beautiful
Years that could have made me beautiful
Had someone cared for me
But now I am only a gnarled tree,
Broken and stunted.

7

THE HOME FRONT
IN WARTIME

The first four years of my life are flickering blurred black and white newsreels whirring away in my mind.

I must have been about two years old. Shaw had arranged for a brief meeting at the British Museum during a break in the bombing. A figure I now know to be my father leaned into my pushchair, touching me fleetingly on the cheek.

Marion kept the last letter she received from Morris. It is dated 7 October 1942.

It seems I should be giving much more consideration to Peter's future than I have done in the past, partly due to preoccupation with other things and partly because I thought matters were best left as they were.

He and Shaw had agreed upon an arrangement committing Morris to pay twenty-four pounds per year to my upkeep until I was fourteen. The fund was to be administered by Shaw who Morris said,

…is so much more reliable and steady and his position so much more assured than either yours or mine that this arrangement could not be bettered.

Four months later, Morris and his new wife Mary had their first child, a girl, Gillian. The second, David, was born three years after that. Morris had been honest with Mary about his past and she had been more tolerant than many of her generation would have been in those circumstances. The provision of the allowance to Marion allowed them to put the past behind them honourably. They agreed they would not tell anyone of my existence. In theory, that was the end of the matter. In practice, Morris did not let go entirely. Shaw continued to provide him with regular bulletins about my plodding progress towards adulthood.

I was too young to be aware of all the machinations of the adults. Mum told me my father had been killed in an air raid whilst he was ushering his class into an air raid shelter during one of the early bombing raids. I didn't know what I was supposed to feel about that. I didn't miss him at all. Red Hill provided a steady supply of male influences, although some of those may have been of doubtful quality.

Another picture. Red Hill, 1944. I was about four years old. The Battle of Britain had been fought and won in the skies above the school. London was still facing attack from the air. The V1 flying bombs (often called 'doodlebugs' or 'buzzbombs' by Londoners) were being launched from France towards London, the south east and elsewhere. These were terrifying weapons. The signature of a doodlebug, recognisable even to a four year old, was the sound of an engine noise switching off, a brief silence, and then a tremendous bang as it hit the ground. According to the *Kent Messenger*, ten doodlebugs fell or were shot down around Sutton Valence in a few months during the summer of 1944.

The move to Worcester had not eventuated. Mum and I still visited Barrington Road every six months or so to visit her mother, who had remained there with Agnes and George. She didn't see any reason why the prospect of bombing should prevent us going up to London, but Red Hill would always be home to me.

Mum was good at made up stories – all fantasy, goblins and happy endings. I remember her carrying me down the passage to the room I shared with one of the boys, Tom. My bed by the wall was under the print of a tattooed Māori warrior. I don't know how or why the warrior ended up on that particular wall.

Tom, who was about ten, had his bed by the window. After Mum tucked me up, she left, switching off the light and quietly closing the door. Soon, there was the shuddering sound of aircraft up in the night sky outside. Tom sat up and drew the curtain.

"Jesus Christ, Pete, look at *that*," he said as a searchlight flashed across the night sky and briefly flooded our little room with light. He didn't talk down to me, although it must have been a severe trial sharing his room with a four year old. The other children usually called me Pete, POF or even Popcorn, which was Mum's name for me. I preferred Pete. It was more grown up. "That's the Maidstone battery," Tom said, giving me credit for knowing where Maidstone was and what a battery did. "They must be trying to stop the buggers getting to London. Hope they shoot one down. Might be able to find some shrapnel like we did last time."

I was usually included in the boys' explorations around the surrounding fields, which generally followed fighter activity in the sky. I already had a small collection of the burnt metal pieces that were sometimes used as currency in the trading activity that went on within the school. I became quite good at trading shrapnel for comics, although I doubt I got the deals some of the older boys got. You couldn't trade with the girls; they didn't appreciate the magic of shrapnel or its value.

I was not interested in the battle going on in the sky outside. There had been a few of those recently, and in any case, there were more disturbing things happening inside the room. Each time the light flashed through the window it picked out the picture of the alien tattooed face above my bed. Mum had explained to me that he was a good man, that chief. "Anyway," she said "he died a long time ago in a faraway place on the other side of the world." Yet I was not convinced and crawled down into the bed, pulling the rough blanket over my head, safe from the knowing eyes of the chief. One day, I would come to recognise him as Eruera Patuone, Rangatira of the Ngāpuhi tribe of New Zealand.

That night, I just wished Mum would take his picture away.

How I managed to cling to a belief in Father Christmas whilst sharing a room with a worldly ten year old, was a miracle in itself. On Christmas mornings during and just after the war, there was the provocative weight on my bed and I reached down to the clean grey woollen sock, bulging with fruit and sweets. Tom, like many of the Red Hill children, had no stable home to go to for the holidays. We compared what was in our socks and made some trades before I padded down the corridor to Mum's room. Tom went off to one of the larger boys' dorms across the landing to wait for the Christmas breakfast. Mum and I went through Father Christmas' sock once more before we joined the rest of the school who were crowding into the oak-panelled dining room. Weak winter sunlight filtered through the dusty leaded windows. Tables were arranged in a square with piles of parcels for each child there.

"Here's your pile, Pete. Over here by the Christmas tree." One of the bigger boys beckoned me over to my place and I let go of Mum's hand. As the youngest there, the other children treated me as some sort of mascot although Mum was careful to see I was not overindulged. My pile was the same size as everyone else's. Mum made sure I didn't receive anything particularly flash. I happily tore into the packages before me, keeping my eye on what everyone else might be getting. I knew this was just the beginning for me. The day after Boxing Day, we would go off to Barrington Road for a few days like we always did, war or no war. Then there would be more presents.

Apart from Agnes, all of Mum's sisters had married and moved out of the East End. They ended up in Ilford, just a mile or so from Barrington Road but some distance up the social scale. Grace married Steve, the boy next door, and Hilda married Cecil, who worked at the local council. Agnes, the eldest, was next. She married George, a widower who played in the Salvation Army band, but she and George stayed at Barrington Road to look after her mother. May was soon to follow Hilda and Grace. She married Arthur Allcroft, the slightly feckless insurance salesman. Marion was approaching forty and still unmarried.

Those visits to Barrington Road in my early years are more worn, fraying monochrome newsreels in my mind. I see war, excitement and danger, all emanating from the sky. In Kent, the sky provided a backdrop for set-piece air battles for my entertainment and shrapnel for my collection, with no thought of lives lost or bodies mutilated. The war seemed a lot closer, noisier and more dangerous when we got up to London. Mum was always checking where I was. She didn't do that at Red Hill, where I was allowed to roam wherever I wanted to, playing with whoever had the patience to put up with me.

In London during the day, if there were no air raids, 32 Barrington Road was a safe friendly house. At night, it took on a more frightening aspect, even when the skies were quiet. The lights from the marshalling yards at the back threw flickering phantom shadows on the ceiling of the box room I slept in. The candlelit outside toilet was a major hazard fuelled by my overstimulated imagination. I was never quite sure what might be behind the creaking door. It was always a dilemma whether I should leave the door open for a quick exit or close it behind me, putting me at the mercy of whatever may be hiding in there. I was often in trouble for splashing the wooden bench seat, as keeping my aim straight was always a secondary consideration to keeping my eye on what may be coming through, or under, the door behind me. Also outside, the concrete air raid shelter dominated the dark of the tiny garden. I would only go in there accompanied by the grown-ups when the air raid sirens screeched out their warnings. A cluster of grey, ungainly barrage balloons were tethered to the wasteland at the end of the road. The balloons were supposed to confuse low-flying enemy aircraft looking to target the railway yards that ran along the back of Barrington Road. There was something vaguely threatening, rather than protective, about the balloons' elephantine presence swaying silently over us.

One night, we all hurried into the shelter as soon as the sirens sounded. Mary, who by then was Grandma to me, was determined to remain inside the house as she always did during the raids. She had brought up all her kids in 32 Barrington Road and seen out some of the worst bombing of the war there. She was tired of being pushed around. With the others moving quickly towards the shelter Grandma stayed put at her seat at the dinner table. "I'm not going to no shelter for nobody. Anyway, I've not finished my supper," she said, pointing to her warm toast with the pork fat dripping onto it.

"Sounds like Barking is copping it." I recognised Uncle George's voice from the lower bunk of the shelter, his face illuminated by the glowing cigarette in his fingers and the candle on the tea chest that doubled as a table. George was my favourite uncle, a gentle quiet man with the smell of the printing works about him. I liked the way he sat in his armchair in the front room, conducting his imaginary Salvation Army band, using compressed vibrating lips to make the various noises of the instruments as they responded to his phantom baton. When I was old enough, I used to help him wind up the clocks. After the war, it was Uncle George who took me to the terraces at Upton Park, touching off a lifetime and generally unrewarding fascination with football and the fortunes of West Ham United. It was at Upton Park I was able to watch Uncle George morph from the mild man he was at home into a fan, full of vituperative wit, shouting all sorts of crude insults at the referee and the opposition.

"Let's hope they're after the docks again. Them trains are a bit too close for comfort for me." Aunty Agnes was referring to the clattering marshalling yards at the back of the house, a frequent target for the German bombs.

Outside the shelter, searchlights pierced the reddening night sky as the ground shook around us. Mum was with me on the top bunk. Like George, she was smoking. She pulled me towards her, arms encircling me. I snuggled into her prickly warm dressing gown, clutching my Mickey Mouse gas mask, innocent of the implications of the risk that it represented. I was always aware of the apprehension oozing from the adults, which hovered inside the shelter and slithered down the sweating dark walls. Mum held me close. George's glasses glinted in the candlelight as he looked helplessly to the roof of the shelter as if he could see through it and track the path of imminent destruction.

The shaking ground, the howling of the sirens, the screaming silence when the engine of a doodlebug cut out prior to smashing to the ground are the stuff of nightmares to me still. Following the lead of the adults, I was in denial. Like them, I convinced myself that we would not be hit. It was like counting the seconds between thunder and lightning; frightening at first but sure to go away. Bombs happened to other people. Anyway, I was confident that nothing could possibly happen while Mum held me close.

George was right, Barking did cop it that night, but a stray bomb also took out a terraced house round the corner from us. It must have been that bomb that shook 32 Barrington Road and had the temerity to loosen a piece of ceiling plaster into Grandma's dripping toast, while the rest of us crouched in the safety of the shelter. It is that story that grew in the telling but will always remain with me, as it was the first time I had seen Grandma laugh, head thrown back, tears running down her face at the ludicrousness of it all. No wonder I felt that we were indestructible.

The air raids didn't interfere with our Christmases. I always had the Red Hill Christmas celebration first. Then I had another one that the family would lay on especially for Mum and me. Agnes bustled away in the tiny kitchen and soon the warm smell of roast chicken permeated the whole house. There was stuffing, bread sauce and roast spuds. Some of George's Brussels sprouts were coaxed from their frozen stalks for the occasion. Agnes called me in for a taste of the pudding. I also sampled the marzipan she was making for the cake that we would have on New Year's Eve. I didn't like the sickly almond taste but I smacked my lips over it dutifully. Hilda and Grace turned up with their children in tow and we all somehow crowded into the front room. My cousin Jo, who had been downstairs when I was born, was maturing, already unaware of the impact of her burgeoning beauty. The other cousin, Sheila, was more my age so I was less intimidated in her presence and we played happily together, although she was not interested in my version of some of the games I had learned from the Red Hill boys.

George was too old to be involved with the war work or home

defences, so he and I were the only males in the house most of the time. He was not at all fazed by that and launched quietly into his Christmas selection conducting *Oh Come, All Ye Faithful* with his imaginary Salvation Army band while Mum and Grandma sipped cups of tea with a bit of 'Christmas' added. Even I knew this was code for tea with increasing amounts of brandy poured into the cup. May was also there. She didn't have children of her own, but hers was the present that I left until last to open as I knew it would have been chosen with great care. After dinner, with the crackers pulled and the paper hats perched uncomfortably on the adults' heads, everything stopped for *ITMA,* the weekly comedy programme on the wireless. Most of the humour was beyond me but the adults' laughter was infectious. I was allowed to stay up for the nine o'clock news. If there were no air raids, the aunties wanted to get home to their husbands in Ilford before it got too late. Each one of them gave me a hug, and after they left, I always found three half-crowns slipped separately into the pockets of my jacket and trousers.

Grandma was probably the only really stable person in Mum's life so it must have been a shock for Mum when she heard about her mother's stroke. Nobody told me what it was but Grandma discarded her long black dress, left her seat by the window and took to her bed. When we visited for Christmas, a huge bed had taken over the parlour and she held court there, patiently waiting for whatever God had in store for her. Marriage to Thomas, losing children to tuberculosis, being missing in action and emigration, and herself surviving the blitz had all etched their pain on her tired old face.

I remember the old lady looking down on me from an enormous bed. I tried hard to imagine her standing upright or even sitting on the carved, bow-legged commode that stood by the bed. She sometimes took her teeth out of the glass beside the bed and popped them into her mouth before talking. As with everything she did, I was never sure whether she wanted me to laugh or be scared. As she got wearier, her false teeth lay discarded on the bedside table, smiling up at their owner. When she wanted me to go the shops for her, she would make a smacking noise with her mouth and search around to see where I was.

"Are y'there, boy?" she asked.

"Yes, Gran," I replied, putting the lid down on the commode and standing on it so she could see me.

She looked at me fiercely as she struggled to focus her eyes and span the years between us. "Go round to the corner shop and get me snuff. There's a bob on the side there. Just say you want your Grandma's special. They'll know what to give you. Keep the change for them gobstoppers you like."

The treat in these trips was not so much the gobstoppers as watching Grandma being helped to sit up in bed so she could eagerly empty the packet of snuff into her special tin. She would then pick at the sharp smelling powder, carefully placing pinches on the back of her hand before noisily snorting some up each nostril in turn. She'd then waggle her nose, sneeze vigorously and settle back onto her pillows with a grunt of pleasure.

Grandma eventually got taken off to Whipps Cross Hospital in Leytonstone. My last memory is of her beached and snuff-less in her hospital bed. Mum, May and Agnes were talking over the figure on the bed as if she wasn't there. Grandma didn't seem to mind.

"Let's have a look then," Agnes said as she drew back the covers. A warm rotting smell escaped from the bedclothes. She turned to Mum. "You're the nurse. What do y'think?"

I sensed Mum putting herself between the bed and me but she wasn't quick enough. I caught sight of the large grey thigh and the ragged muslin. While the attention of the grown-ups was occupied examining where the leg should have been, I turned and looked curiously towards the head on the pillows. I knew from what they said in the bus on the way to the hospital that the old lady was going to die. I'd heard a lot about dead people during the war, but I'd never seen one. I leaned forward curiously. Grandma's eyes flicked open, and she frowned that frown of hers.

"What is it boy? Thought your Gran had gone did yer?" There was no answer to that. She chuckled to herself, muttered something about winning a three-legged race and then dismissed me by simply closing her eyes. I looked up at Mum. I'd never seen her cry before. Grandma died a few weeks later. She was eighty-two.

Without Grandma as the focal point, the family began to fragment. Agnes reigned at number 32 with George as her loyal consort. Mum and I continued to visit at Christmas or at any other time she could get away from Red Hill. The identity of my father remained a mystery to the rest of the family, but I was accepted as one of them. Mum always referred to Barrington Road as 'home', but to me it was just somewhere we went at Christmas time or when Mum could get time off. As far as I was concerned, Red Hill School was my home.

8

A NORMAL UPBRINGING

Throughout my early childhood, I shared a dorm, ate and played with and was subject to the same rules as the other boys at Red Hill, so it did not occur to me not to attend any of the school activities that were going on around me. If I was resented as 'MOF's boy', I was blissfully unaware of it. Red Hill was my home. It never closed for school holidays and my routines and interactions with the other boys did not change, even when, later, I was required to attend more conventional schools.

Mum was allocated a bedroom by the main stairs so she was the centre of all the action and handy to the bedwetters' dorm. I ended up in the upper attic dorm, which I shared with two older boys. One of these Ralph Gee, has since told me he was very pleased when MOF told him he had been allocated this dorm, as it was quiet and out of the way. He said MOF left him in no doubt that he had been carefully selected and MOF, personally, would be keeping a strict eye on him. From the age of five, I had learned to stake out my own territory in the small attic room, and special books and toys were always at hand. My two room-mates were equally territorial about their space but tolerated the presence of someone half their age. I was usually asleep by the time they came to bed but sometimes I listened in to their conversations. In the mornings, I would negotiate the steep stairs down to the main landing where Mum's room was located and get ready for the day. It would start with breakfast with everyone else in the main dining room. From then on, my day was my own.

In his book *Maladjusted Boys,* Shaw described the selection process employed at Red Hill. He was very clear that the minimum IQ level acceptable was 130. Beyond that, he was very open to accepting boys from highly disturbed backgrounds, some of whom had been before the courts. He appears to have drawn the line at any identifiable psychopathic behaviour in those he accepted. Some did not know their parents; others may have wished their parents dead. Many had seen and experienced violence within their home that had left them physically and emotionally damaged. At least one boy had witnessed a murder within the family. Some were simply victims of wartime bombing.

Mum was very discreet when talking to me about the boys I was playing with. Occasionally I would find myself under cross examination from one of the boys.

"Where's your dad then, Pete?" This from a ten year old in the casual manner of young boys who exchanged confidences rather in the way we exchanged cigarette cards of footballers and film stars. On this particular day we were sorting out conkers. His world-beating fifty-fiver, probably enhanced by a good soaking in vinegar, was up against my paltry sixer.

"Died in the war. Never met him." I was still trotting out what I believed to be the truth. I waited for the boy to reciprocate with information but it would not matter if he didn't. Red Hill boys tended to be quite guarded about their home life. Shaw maintained he would respect and jealously guard any confidences he was entrusted with. He certainly jealously guarded the secret surrounding my parentage.

"Mine used to kick the shit out of me. Never came back from the war. Mum disappeared too, so I come here." It was a familiar story and no elaboration was offered. We got on with stringing up our conkers.

I was the only staff child that lived in the school itself. Shaw had moved from a bungalow in the village to a large house, Millfield House, on the road to Sutton Valence. Mum had retained her friendship with Shaw's wife, Joan. Mum and I frequently walked the two miles over the fields to visit them at Millfield, usually when Shaw was not there. Timothy, their eldest child, was slightly younger than me. Tim and I used to play and ride our bikes together but he rarely came to Red Hill itself. Tim was a bright quiet boy. His younger sister Carol was clearly her mother's daughter – vivacious, with long blonde hair and clear blue eyes. I did not see much of Kevin, the youngest, but as he grew up, he had the reputation in the village of an engaging tearaway.

Ren'chen was the eldest daughter of Lily and Ivor Holland, Shaw's deputy principal. They had a cottage in the grounds at Red Hill. Ren'chen was about my age. She and I used to play together on occasions, although I wasn't really used to having girls to play with. There was tennis on the lawn and sometimes doctors and nurses in the bushes by the front gate until we were caught at that by one of the Red Hill boys. Any lasting friendship between us was inhibited by the acrimonious relationship that existed between our parents. Time had not healed whatever had gone on between Mum and Lily in the early days. Ren'chen went away to school. She came back in the holidays a beautiful young woman and was soon attracting lots of attention whenever she appeared on the front lawn outside the Hollands' cottage in the grounds.

School prefects were known as Bench Members and junior prefects as Citizens. These continued to be elected by the school community and heard grievances and some breaches of school discipline at the weekly school court in the large panelled dining room. The court ruled upon convictions and decided upon suitable sanctions for the miscreants, often guided by precedents that had begun to accumulate. The court proceedings were taken very seriously, and there was a formality to them, which was respected. I loved the drama of it all and usually sat quietly with a group of the younger boys watching Red Hill justice being meted out.

There were usually up to ten cases heard at each sitting. A typical exchange would be:

Smythe: "I charge Neville Baker with swearing at me yesterday on the bus from Maidstone to the detriment of public relations."

Court: "Have you anything to say, Neville?"

Baker: "I did tell Smythe to 'fuck off', but I was provoked."

Court: "Any witnesses?"

Smith: "I was there. Baker did shout out but only after Smythe grabbed hold of his balls in continuance of a play fight that had started before we got on the bus. I didn't think it was very serious and there were no members of the public present."

Court (after consideration): "We find the charge proven. We warn both Smythe and Baker about their behaviour in public in future. If there is any further incidence of swearing or fighting in public by either then a fine or gating (confined to school grounds for a period) will be imposed."

Fines were recorded against the offender's account and paid into the community fund or to the aggrieved party as directed by the court. The accounting side was handled by Morley Gayton, whose skill and patience as a teacher fitted him well for the role as accountant to the court. Shaw and most of the staff were present at the court but they seldom intervened in the process unless invited to do so by the court. Outside the court, staff still had some sanctions available to them, although some of these could be appealed in court. With one or two exceptions, Shaw's commitment not to resort to any form of corporal punishment held firm.

With fifty or so highly intelligent but mostly disturbed boys herded together there were games, obsessions and behaviours that were completely outside what would be understood or accepted in conventional boarding schools. Sometimes Mum would be involved with sorting out bruised and broken limbs resulting from tree-jumping competitions or cleaning and stitching wounds received from brick-heaving contests. There were not many days that went by without her opening up the medical room to attend to some wound or another. She was always the one who was called. I was often an interested observer of her at work, whether it was treating an epileptic thrashing around in a pool of blood from a fall or calming some boy convinced he had been bitten by an adder. Grigglestone was a tough young lad who, for some reason, fell out with Shaw. Inevitably, Mum took him under her wing, and he has memories of spending many hours in her room smoking and chatting or listening to the wireless. Grigglestone was particularly admired for his ability to head a cricket ball continuously for a minute, although some of these sessions would end up in the medical room. Another boy had to be treated after spectacularly losing a battle with wasps during a summer's long campaign against their nests.

Any rare case of physical bullying was dealt with by the court. Differences of opinions between boys were usually sorted out by argument rather than fists. The frisson of sexual excitement that simmered over Red Hill when the girls were there had subsided after Red Hill became a boys-only school in 1947. Sex was freely discussed, and some of the games of rough and tumble had a sexual component but, as I was to find out, no more than at any other all-male institution.

Indoor games centred on various Red Hill versions of conventional card games, which sometimes lasted for hours. Red Hill versions of Monopoly and Cluedo were developed. Whole week-long competitions were set up around Subbuteo table soccer in which the players used their fingers to flick plastic figures around a green baize table. Table tennis, snooker and billiards tournaments were organised, taking weeks to complete. It was all very fair and I was often given a handicap to compensate for my age and size, although this was withdrawn as I got older.

I used to watch uncomprehendingly while some of the older boys smoked and played bridge, which was one game that maintained its integrity in the Red Hill environment. For some reason, I never got around to smoking although many of the Red Hill boys smoked. Dog-ends, picked up following staff meetings, were often used as a sort of currency.

The dusty square behind the bike sheds had been used by the

gardeners at Charlton Court to store the wood for the fires and boilers in the main house. The woodpile, as it was called, was springy underfoot from the old wood chippings but it provided a forgiving surface for a whole range of specially adapted games, including inventive versions of football where participants represented their favourite teams. Arsenal, Liverpool and the usual glamour teams were there, along with less fashionable clubs: Notts Forest, Barrow and even St Albans City. I, of course, took on the responsibility for representing West Ham United, which had as much success on the woodpile as they did at Upton Park.

The surrounding countryside was also safe to explore. Sutton Valence, the pretty village overlooking the Weald of Kent, was about thirty minutes' walk from the school. To reach Sutton Valence you had to pass the Church of St Peter and St Paul. A church has been on that site since Saxon times, and parts of the present ragstone building date back to the Normans. The graveyard is positioned on each side of the road and is full of crumbling graves and monuments. It was a threatening place to walk through, particularly at night when the wind hummed through the hop wires and bats swooped out of the tower. One peeled and pitted headstone still has the words *Remember me as you pass by. As you are now, so once was I* chipped out on its surface. Sometimes one of the bigger boys would take me to Sutton Valence on the crossbar of his bike. When I was older I had my own bike. Whether I walked or was on my bike, I was well into my teens before I went past East Sutton church at night without closing my eyes tight shut.

Many of the games, practical jokes and other deceptions were reprised each year on April Fools' Day. Mum's area was often the target as bedding was hidden, cupboards barricaded and even, once, her own room made inaccessible. She didn't pull rank, but one year she told me of her plan to outflank the pranksters by hiding some mats in her own room overnight and declaring that breakfast would not be served until whoever had hidden the mats put them back. The whole school was in uproar. I was bursting with the secret she had shared with me but kept my mouth shut. After two hours she calmly produced the mats and breakfast was served. She was left alone after that. She frequently found herself at odds with Shaw over his involvement in some pranks that got out of hand. One particular incident I observed was when a couple of boys, with Shaw's active encouragement, stole the clothes of MOF's young assistant from outside the staff bathroom. I was an enthralled bystander watching Betty, the young assistant, in tears at the bottom of the stairs trying to cover herself. Mum was screaming invective at Shaw to, among other things, get "Betty's fucking clothes back. Now!" She was usually quite careful about swearing when I was around, but Shaw had gone too far on that occasion and the clothes were quickly returned.

Red Hill became known as a place that accepted boys other institutions would not touch. More than that, the regime was getting good results. This gave Shaw a better platform from which to recruit staff. Paul Pollack and Len Bloom, both ex-pupils, stayed for some time as teachers. Audrey Davies was taken on during the fifties. She told me she met Shaw at a party and he simply said, "Come and work for me." She was not long out of Oxford and was looking for just the type of experience that Red Hill would provide. Many of the younger staff Shaw recruited were not seeking long-term employment, although some did stay at Red Hill for five or six years. Shaw had a good eye for talent and Audrey fitted very much into the mould of people he liked to take on. She was extremely bright, interested in teaching in its widest possible sense, and was a bit of a risk taker. She thought I was a serious little boy, which I would have been in the presence of such a vivacious and outgoing person. She remembers MOF as a tough cookie with a bitter sardonic humour covering a lot of warmth.

Most of the staff tolerated my presence as I sat in at various staff meetings. I found that sitting quietly in the corner, I could pick up some quite interesting gossip. I remember Mum once interrupting a fascinating discussion about the transgressions of a recently departed colleague. She noticed me taking it all in. "Watch out," she said, moving her head in my direction. "There are some big ears in the corner!"

Similarly, I attended the classes that took my fancy or ones Mum thought I should go to. I spent hours in the art room with Bob Payne, the art teacher. Bob had a very practical approach to art. He encouraged participation in a wide range of activities and most boys found something in the art room that was interesting. I worked on papier-mâché masks, and enjoyed chipping out rudimentary figures from stone. Art, craft, writing and performance were all brought together in Bob's Magic Theatre puppet group. Works on paper were often an outlet to express previously repressed fantasies and disturbing dreams which Shaw would sometimes include in his therapy sessions. Output from Bob's classes began to find an outlet at the Cooling Gallery in Albemarle Street in London where the works of Red Hill boys were regularly exhibited.

Bob was a gentle man with a soothing West Country burr. He had been at sea on Atlantic convoys during the war and, as a result of his experiences, had become a pacifist. From him, I learned to mistrust film portrayals of wartime exploits involving Richard Todd, Kenneth More, Jack Hawkins and other actors with stiff upper lips. Mum would not take me to western films, and Bob's wife also refused to go. Bob's pacifist principles did not extend to Gary Cooper and Henry Fonda, and he was happy to use me as an excuse to go along to the Granada in Maidstone to see films like *High Noon, Fort Apache* and *My Darling Clementine.*

Otto Shaw *was* Red Hill School, from the time he established the school until his death in 1976. Like many charismatic leaders he attracted loyal followers and some detractors. The gauche young man who interviewed Mum all those years ago was still evident. He remained awkward around women. The incident with Betty on the stairs was symptomatic of immature, if not misogynistic behaviour, although this does need to be put in the context of the times.

Shaw took great care to cultivate the local community and Red Hill had remarkably little trouble from police, local farmers and community leaders as a result. An eloquent and energetic member of the Labour Party, Shaw stood and was defeated in three general elections: first in Maidstone in 1945; then in Thanet in 1951; and finally in Maidstone in 1955. These were all safe Tory seats, which is just as well, as it is unlikely that he could have combined being an MP with running Red Hill.

I have no memory at all of the ending of the war and how it was celebrated but I do remember very clearly the 1945 general election. These were bewildering and exciting times for a five year old squeezed in the back of Shaw's Wolseley, carefully keeping score of the number of houses displaying 'Vote Labour. Vote Shaw' posters in sitting room windows. Sometimes I would be taken along with other Red Hill boys to village halls to hear him debate with the Tory candidate, the unfortunate Alfred Bossom. Even I could see how Shaw could hold an audience and put down his opponent with wit and sheer force of personality.

He clearly relished this exposure and soon he was surfacing in all sorts of roles and local committees. He was also attracting media attention at the local and national level.

On 16 August 1949, *The Times* described Shaw as 'the well-known lay psychotherapist' when quoting him at length on the subject of art therapy for the reform of delinquents. He was appointed as a magistrate and frequently heard minor criminal cases as chair of the local bench. The *Kent Messenger* always knew there would be some entertainment and a quote or two to be had when Otto Shaw was presiding.

Only someone with Shaw's energy and self-confidence could combine such an exhausting public life with the demands of running Red Hill School. I admired him greatly but was intimidated by him. I was grateful to him for the support he gave to Mum and to me. As I grew older, I began to resent the control he seemed to have over us.

9

THE AUTHORITIES
INTERVENE

The freedoms enjoyed by Shaw, A.S. Neill at Summerhill, and other leaders of the progressive school movement were pulled into line by the passing of the Education Act in 1944. For Red Hill to receive referrals from local education authorities, it would have to conform to the Education Act. The Ministry was probably influential in having the school closed to girls in 1947. Mum kept in touch with a few of the girls after they left, but soon their presence faded into Red Hill folklore.

In February 1950 the school was visited by HM Inspectors, all ten of them, from the Ministry of Education. Unfortunately, a boy at the school chose the second day of the inspectors' visit to take an axe to a teacher. It was a dreadful assault and quite without precedent in the colourful history of Red Hill. Mum was involved in treating the teacher and getting him off to hospital. From the report they issued, the inspectors appear to have responded to the situation with reasonable equanimity. An attempt by the inspectors to fit Red Hill into the bland reporting template they were used to seems to have posed some difficulties for them. Their report identified some minor problems and was critical of some of the teaching practices and aspects of the school court process.

The inspectors acknowledged that the Red Hill regime, for all the faults observed, was succeeding in its basic role of stabilising the lives of many of the boys. Shaw would have been reasonably pleased with the report but he would not have been aware of a highly confidential addendum that was attached to the report. Whether it was the assault or whether the inspectors approached Red Hill with a particular agenda in mind is not clear, but the addendum was scathing in its criticism of Shaw.

The inspector who wrote the addendum expressed doubt about Shaw's claim to a PhD and other qualifications. He questioned Shaw's professional and personal qualifications to undertake psychoanalysis, claiming that *'The Principal is himself suffering from psychological difficulty.'* Shaw's ability to manipulate and charm civil servants must have let him down on this occasion.

The confidential addendum goes on:

Every Inspector who has met the Principal had formed a most unfortunate opinion of him and especially of his attempt to shock by discussing without reserve aberrations in sexual behaviour and the disguised manifestations of this in his pupils' art and writing.

And a few paragraphs later:

…he has a feeling of inferiority when with professional or educated people. Being a complete extrovert, his personality is displeasing to many, and it was noticeable that each member of a large inspecting panel found him unpleasant. I think an expression of this inferiority is his choice of a room at the top of the house, with two doors so low that all entering his presence must bow down as they do so. Also, his choice of a large collection of books about Napoleon and of prints of the Napoleonic wars, led me to wonder if he was inclined to identify himself with Napoleon, the emperor.

The addendum ends with the following more conciliatory passage:

His treatment appears to be more intuitive than reasoned. I have spoken to Dr (Alan) Maberly since my visit, and he agrees that Shaw does get good results also that he will admit more severely maladjusted boys than most other schools. He thinks that Shaw has considerable intuition into these boys' needs, that he works hard, and drives others to help them and that it cannot be denied that good work is being done for this type of boy. He (Maberly) does not think that his psychotherapeutic methods are capable of harming any boy.

It seems likely that Shaw did overstate, or even lie about, his professional qualifications, and that is unforgivable for someone in his position. As to the revelations about the darker side of his character, it seems that Her Majesty's Inspectors were not above making snap subjective judgements themselves, based on personal antipathy. If they really felt they had a case against Shaw they would surely have seen to it that he was confronted with their full findings, and had him removed. They would have known that without him as principal, Red Hill would almost certainly have had to close.

The inspectors could have saved themselves a lot of trouble if they had talked to Mum or to some of the boys about Shaw. Yes, he was a show-off, obsessed with his own power and ability to control. Yes, he was uncomfortable with women and was sexist, even by the standards that existed at the time. However, Mum would have said that there were other, more important aspects to his character. He was not one to take himself too seriously, was generous, and enjoyed and encouraged debate. Critically, his leadership of Red Hill provided a pathway that changed the lives of many who went through the place. Mum worked with Major Faithfull at Hazeleigh Lodge, so she knew what a charlatan looked like. Shaw was no charlatan in the Faithfull mode. Mum made Shaw my legal guardian, which describes very well the relationship she (and I) had with him. I was always timid and inarticulate around him, but I never doubted that he cared for Mum and for me as he oversaw my stumbling, plodding progress to adulthood.

My education had been limited to taking part in the community life at Red Hill, supplemented on occasions by going along to more formal classes in the main school building that Mum thought I should attend. Somehow, the Kent Education authorities had found out that there was a 'normal' six year old child being brought up in the abnormal and potentially damaging Red Hill community. In 1946, it was made clear to Mum that I must attend the village school. My attendance at Sutton Valence Primary School was my first exposure to formal schooling in post-war England.

The eccentric community that was Red Hill did not prepare me well for conventional schooling. The quaint but effective democracy applied at Red Hill was replaced by a more authoritarian regime at the primary school. I was not used to treating adults with deference rather than as equals. The teachers at my new school did not react well to being told by one of their young charges that he was "bursting for a piss". I also got into trouble for taking cigarettes to school. I thought I might be able to get a good trade for shrapnel, which was still being picked up in the Kent countryside two years after the war.

The Kent Education authorities were unimpressed with my slow progress at Sutton Valence Primary School. I struggled to keep joined-up writing legible, and spelling within the realms of the possible. Arithmetic was a desert of incomprehension stretching far into the distance. After a few terms of non-achievement, it was time for the authorities to step in once more. I was nearly eight years old. Mum had her instructions and would not have been looking forward to giving me the bad news. She chose school report time to tackle the issue.

"This is not a great school report again, darling, although they do say you try hard and are quite good at football. Miss Morgan says that your work is untidy and you have far too much to say for yourself." I had already pitted my wits against Miss Morgan and complained to Mum about the teacher's lack of fairness. It was clear that Mum, in a strange contradiction to her own approach, would never support me in challenging authority, however justified my complaints might be. "You have to be careful with women that age," she said, trying to explain away Miss Morgan's aggression. "So many had husbands who were killed in the war, and it's very hard for them." That effectively shut me up.

The report was no worse than previous ones, and usually she would find something we could laugh about in the pedantic condescending words. Not this time.

"The education people have decided that living here at Red Hill and mixing with Red Hill boys can't be good for you." I looked at her to see if I could find a clue in her face that would help me understand what that meant or what was coming. There was nothing there.

She talked as if she was trying to remember her lines. "They have said that you have to go away from here to a proper school, although you can come home to Red Hill in the holidays." She spoke quickly.

I didn't understand what was being said or what a 'proper school' might be, but I knew from the way she was saying it that this was not good news at all. "Do you mean I'm to be sent to an orphanage or an approved school?" I had picked up enough from the Red Hill boys to know some of the options that were open to authorities if there were problems at home.

"No love, nothing like that. But you will have to go to a boarding school at least until you can sit the eleven plus." Already, the exam that I would have to sit in a few years' time was looking like an insurmountable hurdle to me. I knew what a boarding school was. It was not the same as an approved school, but it would still mean I was going to be sent away.

"Shaw has got you into Eltham College where he went when he was a boy."

I supposed I was expected to be grateful, but I had no concept then of what sort of influence Shaw would have brought to bear with the Kent Education Committee, or with the Eltham College, to get me into Eltham as a boarder. Shaw was on the school board of Eltham.

In fact, Shaw had been very influential as he had been throughout my early life. I have a letter to the County Education Officer that he had drafted for Mum to copy and sign in her handwriting, arguing the case for my placement at Eltham. Tellingly, Mum had queried a sentence in Shaw's draft letter as it made reference to her parlous financial state, particularly the fact she was in receipt of a small sum being paid into an insurance policy by a friend – presumably this referred to Morris's payments. "Is it absolutely necessary to include this?" she asked.

Eltham was then a minor public school originally set up for the sons of missionaries whose fathers were bringing light to dark exotic places around the world. As I was nearly eight I was to attend the junior school, which was effectively a prep school, grooming boys for the main school. It was only an hour's bus ride from Maidstone, but, to me, that represented a major expedition. More than that, a public school would be a completely different basket of eccentricities and challenges than I was used to at Red Hill.

Finding the money to get me fitted out for the required school uniform was a worry for Mum. All through my time at Eltham, with Shaw acting on her behalf, she engaged in a running battle with the education authorities to get help with expenses that would keep a growing boy kitted out to the exacting levels required. I knew nothing of all this when she took me into G.H. Laveys, the gents' outfitters in Maidstone, to get suited up in uncomfortable, itchy grey serge. I looked sadly into the mirror as she helped me with the yellow and blue striped tie. At the beginning of the September term she travelled with me on the coach to Eltham. Normally I would relish a ride on the coach, but not that time. Red Hill was home to me. The little dorm I was sharing with Ralph Gee and the other boy was my place, and I was happy there. Mum's bedsitter next to the bedwetters was a haven.

On that first day, Mum and I trudged up the sweeping drive towards the junior school at Eltham College. After completing the preliminaries, Mum handed me over to the school matron, kissed me goodbye and turned quickly away. I bit my lip and held back the tears. As she walked down the driveway, I noticed for the first time how small she was. I waited in case she would turn and wave goodbye; she didn't. The matron touched my shoulder and I followed her inside.

I was one of a number of very young boys who were nervously starting the school year at Eltham College that day. As despised 'new bugs', we would remain in that category for at least a term. We were shown around by one of the senior boys and given supper in the dining hall. There was, for me, the familiar smell of disinfectant, floor polish and that peculiar body odour that young boys wear like body armour.

On the surface, it was just like Red Hill, although it lacked the anarchic, world-weary sophistication I was used to. Since I was an old lag as far as institutional living was concerned, I found myself, at seven years old, becoming something of a de facto leader and spokesman for our small group of new bugs. I had not seen any physical bullying at Red Hill, but I was precocious in the ways of institutions and aware that, in any school community, there were risks to newcomers who drew too much attention to themselves. I did not have the size, courage, or verbal dexterity to defend myself should I need to. So I made sure that all my communications with the senior boys, in particular, were deferential, bordering upon the obsequious.

Being in a dormitory with other boys was nothing new to me, but it was the first time I had been away from my mother. After the lights were switched out, the boy in the next bed sobbed quietly into his pillow. Later that night, the sobs turned into deep cries of anguish. I didn't know what to say to him so I ended up making a general announcement to the dorm at large. "I am going to the bog so if anyone wants to come, I'll show you where it is. They won't want you pissing your bed here." I was an expert on the subject, having watched Mum regularly piling up soiled sheets from the bedwetters' dorm. One or two boys followed me sheepishly to the end of the dorm where the toilets were located. After a few nights the crying stopped. I negotiated that first term successfully, but I always looked forward to going home to Red Hill.

I always knew my holidays at my Red Hill home were coming to an end when Mum would say, "Have you been to see Shaw yet? He'll want to say goodbye." Every boy at Red Hill would have some time in Shaw's office at the top of the steep stairs. These were usually for the regular sessions of psychoanalysis. It was there that dreams were analysed, fantasies dissected and anger vented. I was always apprehensive on entering his office through the tiny entrance way that opened into a large carpeted book-lined room. I was not there for psychoanalysis. I think he genuinely wanted to say goodbye to me each time I went back to school. Sitting or standing, he dominated any room he was in. For the 'goodbye' sessions with me he would usually be leaning back in his large chair, smoking his pipe, with hands clasped over an expanding paunch. His loudly checked sports jacket would be draped carelessly over his battered, ever-open and bulging briefcase. Each time I went to see him I was determined not to cry, and each time I failed. Sometimes, I would just sit there weeping uncontrollably while he calmly waited for me to compose myself. As I got older, I handled these meetings better, but I always felt he was waiting for me to reveal something of myself to him. That was what he was used to in that room. Revealing myself to Shaw was something I was initially unable and, eventually, unwilling to do. Each meeting would always end up with him solemnly shaking my hand and handing over some money. By the time I went off to school for the last time, ten shillings passed hands.

For my second term Mum entrusted Reg Slade, a senior Red Hill Bench Member, with the task of taking me up to Eltham. Whether she simply could not get the time off or whether she wanted to ensure, at eight years old, I could manage without her, I am not sure, but I didn't mind. I liked Reg. He remembers me sitting looking quietly out of the bus window. Reg has said that he was very aware that MOF had carefully selected him for the job as escort. He was worried I would do a runner and wondered how he was going to face MOF if that happened. In fact, it was an uneventful journey and he was able to report to MOF that he thought I had travelled well. After that, I travelled to and from Eltham on my own, although there were occasions when Shaw turned up in his Wolseley to bring me home. Shaw's son Timothy later joined me at Eltham. So at ten years old, I was able to give Tim the benefit of my three years' experience of life at boarding school. Tim did not have my problems with the eleven plus examinations so his education took a much different path to mine, and we grew apart.

At Red Hill there was plenty of opportunity to play sport, although often to the rather idiosyncratic rules that sometimes applied. At Eltham I soon excelled at football and cricket, so that made up for my lack of scholastic achievement.

Neither Mum nor Red Hill had prepared me for my encounter with God. Despite the whiff of Catholicism in her own childhood, she was not a religious person and so must have wondered what a school for the sons of missionaries would have in store for me, with its constant diet of muscular Christianity. For a year or two I embraced the Protestant religion with messianic fervour, equalled only by my passion for football. Gaining acceptability within the confines of a public school system was an instinctive goal for me. There was a cost to this. We frequently played cricket against one of the local secondary modern schools. On one occasion, the opposing team turned up on our plush green playing fields with very little equipment. And some of them weren't even in whites! My superiority and condescension knew no bounds. As captain of our group of small boys, I protested to the visitors' teacher about this lack of protocol. How was it possible to play cricket without whites? I was becoming a very good public school boy.

Going home to Red Hill for the school holidays reminded me very graphically of where I was from. Each term I travelled from one extreme of the English education system to the other. The fact that it all seemed so normal to me says much for the matter-of-fact and pragmatic way Mum approached her role as a solo mother.

I duly failed the eleven plus examination and my boarding status at Eltham had to be reviewed. Again Shaw was there, negotiating a compromise with the authorities. I was able to continue at Eltham as a day boy, provided I could be boarded out with a family within walking distance of the school. Shaw arranged for my placement with the Carter family in Crossmead near Eltham. Mrs Carter went to work in the city, and Mr Carter worked on the river in some capacity that was never quite clear to me. They seemed to have an ordered, predictable life. Their eldest son, Barry, had attended Eltham College, and I knew of him as a talented athlete and rugby player. He had left home to join the navy. The other son, Robert, was younger than me and was scheduled to start at Eltham shortly after I arrived in Crossmead. I had managed the transition from Red Hill to public school, but now I was going to see how a conventional middle class family operated. The only experience I had of a life outside an institution was the few days we spent at Barrington Road every year at Christmas time. At Crossmead there seemed to be so many subtle, unspoken and changing rules to deal with, particularly at meal times. Why did you have to wait for everyone to get their food before you could start yours? What was this about asking to leave the table after a meal? Most mystifying of all were the different pieces of cutlery to match the food. As for serviettes, I thought hankies were what you blew your nose on. None of these rules applied at Red Hill or, for that matter, at Eltham.

There was some expectation that I would act as an elder brother to Robert, in the absence of Barry. With the Carters both working, I was to provide some oversight of Robert until they got home, but I did not have the maturity nor tolerance needed for such a role. This was difficult for both of us. Robert was used to having a glamorous elder brother to provide mentoring and advice. I was hardly that. There were conflicts and arguments from time to time, but somehow there were no major dislocations. This was due mainly to the pacifying influence of the television set in the corner of the living room that Robert and I watched avidly from five to six pm every weeknight.

It seemed odd to me, walking off as a day boy to a school where I had spent four years as a boarder. The most difficult aspect of living with the Carters was finding time and space to be on my own. Both at Red Hill and at Eltham it was possible to find time for yourself. I had learned early on at Red Hill that it was important to establish territory. I was not a solitary boy but I was a dreamer who sometimes liked a place in which to dream.

My commitment to God nurtured in the Eltham environment began to waver. I found that it was easy to walk out of school during some of the religious services in the school chapel. A couple of hours walking around the shops and visiting the local library seemed to me a much more interesting use of my time. I finally broke my contract with God when I found that I could please the Carters by asking to go off to church for Sunday service. I didn't go, of course, and spent many a happy Sunday morning roaming around Eltham High Street or watching Sunday morning football in the local park.

The Carters were generous in involving me in all their family activities but that only made me feel even more out of place. Mr Carter once made a half-hearted attempt to teach me to box. This was one sporting activity that made no sense to me. After a couple of hours spent ducking and weaving in the hall at Crossmead, he gave up on me. I was so hopeless he decided not to waste the money on boxing gloves.

In those days, the thirteen plus examination was effectively the last chance saloon educationally. I had by then graduated to the school-age group rugby team at Eltham, so my status within the school remained assured, although being a day boy had dropped me down the pecking order a bit. The Carters continued to try hard to include me in everything, but I simply could not fit in with the life they led. Running away was not an option. Where would I go? Mum knew I was unhappy there, but I tried to keep from her how miserable I really was. I knew enough about our affairs to know there would be nothing she could do about it. It was looking as if I would have to get used to the two-storey semi-detached at Crossmead. Then something fortuitous happened – I failed the thirteen plus.

Passing the thirteen plus could mean entrance into a more technically oriented school, even though I was the least technically minded boy imaginable. Failure would open the trap door into a secondary modern school, which was seen as a bit of a lottery. As I had failed the exam by only a few marks, I would have one further chance to redeem myself. I suspect Shaw would have been involved somewhere.

Mum and I went along to an interview with the Kent Education Authority in Maidstone. A panel of three suited men was lined up on the other side of a shiny table. This was not a situation that Mum had any experience of but she did what she could to prepare me, making sure I was neat and tidy.

"And what do you do when you are at home, Peter? Do you help your mother around the house?" The balding man with his neck bulging over his collar leaned forward invitingly.

I was confused. We didn't live in a house. Didn't he know that? I shifted uncomfortably in my seat, trying to give him the answer he was looking for. In the end I just opted to mumble "Yes."

The next question was about what I wanted to be when I grew up. It was not a subject I had given much thought to as I had happily driven imaginary buses round the grounds of Red Hill or played football on the woodpile.

Using my Red Hill and Eltham experiences, I rolled my answer into what I thought was an acceptable package. "A gentleman farmer," I said brightly. The panel members were unresponsive.

"And what do you know about farming?" the one with the spotted blue bow tie asked.

"I know that Cox's Orange apples rattle when you shake them." I could see that wasn't quite what they were looking for. A cloud of quiet descended upon the room. A panel member coughed; another scribbled furiously into a notebook. The interview stuttered to an uncomfortable conclusion.

Afterwards, Mum and I went for a fish and chip lunch at the Cannon in the town. She must have been disappointed but she did not show it. We laughed as we dissected the interview. We knew I would have been a hopeless farmer and would never make it as a gentleman.

There followed another losing battle with the education authorities to have me retained at Eltham. Shaw once more intervened. I was tested for IQ, Red Hill style, and Shaw attempted unsuccessfully to use those results to relitigate my exam results and poor interview performance. Eventually, Shaw was able to achieve a compromise with the authorities. Always with Shaw, you never quite knew what arm twisting went on behind the scenes to achieve his aims. I would never have survived the education system outside Red Hill without the lobbying he did on my behalf. He arranged for Mum and me to go up to Liverpool to have a look at the Blue Coat School, near Penny Lane in Wavertree.

Shaw took us to Maidstone East Station where we caught the train to London. The four-hour train journey from Euston to Liverpool was the longest journey I had ever undertaken. I didn't realise it then, but Mum had never been on a long-distance train before either. We caught the bus from Lime Street Station to Penny Lane. The impressive red brick frontage of the school was intimidating at first glance, but once we got inside, it was a much more relaxed environment than Eltham's. Mum was particularly impressed with the art room, which resembled Bob Payne's space at Red Hill, with its wide variety of work on show. The teachers we met were interested and friendly. Then we met the Headmaster, Mr Watcyn, a tall Welshman. I had never ever seen Mum so nervous. It was not to do with Watcyn, who was a daunting figure in a gown. It must have been the realisation that this school might actually work for me and that we were running out of options. She was very careful and deferential with Watcyn and fiddled anxiously with her handbag when he turned his attention to me. It must have gone well because within a week of our visit, I was accepted as a boarder at the Blue Coat. It was a second chance of sorts, as the Liverpool Blue Coat School ran two educational streams that enabled late-developing boys to cross over from the secondary modern into the more academic grammar stream of the school.

Although the name of the school, its long tradition in the city, and the imposing building complex indicated otherwise, it was then an unpretentious institution. Boys were sent there from various parts of Lancashire and further afield. Day boys also attended from the local area. Once I overcame the hurdle of my southern accent, Liverpool was a welcoming place and it was good to be away from Crossmead and the claustrophobia that, for me, had gone with family life there. Liverpool was much more of a school community than Eltham, and I soon found myself involved in a whole range of activities. The odd-job man at the Blue Coat, who also did shoe repairs, was called Ted Farrell. His Liverpool accent had been trawled from the depth of the dark and oily Mersey. I had to listen very carefully to identify when he was being serious or when he was taking the piss. In the unimaginative logic of teenage boys, I was given the nickname of 'Ted'. Nicknames were important and not everyone was recognised in this way. I felt accepted and began to pick up on the black humour of my namesake. I even developed my own version of Ted's Liverpool accent.

My scholastic achievements improved in the freer teaching environment that existed at the Blue Coat. Steinbeck, Greene and Orwell, among others, replaced *Charles Buchan's Football Monthly* as my reading material of choice. Poetry and drama no longer appeared to exist in a distant land. I found myself performing in school plays as well as writing what I thought were witty and satirical pieces for the school magazine. At last some aspects of learning were becoming easier for me, although this was Liverpool, and an obsession with sport in general and football in particular was never far away. Sometimes illegal breakout expeditions would be organised to go into the city. It might be to Anfield, to Goodison Park or an X-rated film somewhere or even to the Liverpool Playhouse Theatre. The more sophisticated boys went out to meet up with girls in the park behind the school. The park had long been named "The Mystery" by the locals, as the land had been given to the council by an anonymous donor. It was appropriately named as far as my progress with girls there was concerned.

Many boys came from backgrounds I could understand. Some had only one parent because of the war, marriage breakdown or illegitimacy. I still believed my father died bravely in the Blitz. Once or twice, for table tennis competitions, we divided teams up into 'Bastards versus The Others'. I always played for 'The Others'.

Liverpool was waking from its post-war torpor. Billy Hatton and Brian O'Hara, friends from the Blue Coat, formed a group called The Four Jays, later changed to The Fourmost. Across town, a few ex-Quarry Bank boys set up a skiffle group, The Quarrymen, who later re-formed to become The Beatles.

For school holidays, I exchanged a dormitory at the Blue Coat in Liverpool for the attic dorm at Red Hill, which was my home. Towards the end of my schooling at Liverpool, Mum was allocated a small flat at Red Hill, grandly called the Upper Cottage, above what used to be the stables, a few minutes' walk from the main building. There was a separate room for me, a small bench with a cooking ring, and a toilet for our own use. We still had to go down to the school for a bath.

I enjoyed having my own space. While I was at the Blue Coat, I had been able to maintain limited friendships with some of the Red Hill boys who were then more my age. One of these, John Spiers, remembers coming around to the cottage during my holidays, and he and I planning bike rides around the county. However, I was gradually growing away from Red Hill. My status as 'MOF's boy' began to inhibit those relationships, as I had freedoms to come and go outside the school that they did not. John and others would sometimes break bounds for a spot of illegal drinking or to chase girls in the village. However much I would have liked to have gone on those expeditions, I knew that my involvement would have compromised Mum's position.

10

THE LIE IS SHAKEN OUT

I did not recognise it at the time, but my mother had brought me up to be independent and to make my own way. This, in an environment that must have challenged her at every turn, was draining for her. It showed on her tired, lined face, yet she was strong and I assumed she would always be there to pick me up if I needed it. As I grew up, we talked of most things, but whether by accident or design I do not know, we avoided some of those more personal discussions and confidences that I knew she shared with some of the Red Hill boys who sought her out. We had a love for one another that, on my side, was assumed rather than stated. The only deep personal discussion we ever had, adult to adult, was the one she must have hoped would never happen.

It was 1956, during my last year at the Blue Coat School, when I was still a naïve and uncertain sixteen year old. I was planning a bike ride to Amsterdam with a couple of friends from school. I needed to complete the documentation for a passport. Mum and I were sitting across from one another. I had the half-completed application form open on the small coffee table between us.

"It says here I need my father's details. I just need to put in his full name, where he was born, where he was killed and stuff like that." I looked up.

She smiled tightly and looked blankly at me. For all her considerable strength, she was easily intimidated by bureaucracy. She sighed deeply and got up from her chair.

"Hang on a minute, I need a fag. I'll make us a cup of tea." The panacea for everything. She came back, sat down and put my tea in front of me. She took her time lighting the Player's and then took a long drag. When she spoke, it came in a rush.

"Your father is alive. He was a teacher. Still is. That part's true. He was teaching here at Red Hill but we had to decide what to do once you were on the way. He didn't want to stay with me, so that was that. He left me before you were born." She stubbed out the cigarette and lit another. "His name is Morris Horovitch. Shaw has all the details of where he is now."

"What about the name? Horovitch? That sounds foreign." I wasn't particularly shocked. I really did not know what to feel.

"His parents came from Austria or Poland I think. I never met them. They were Jews. He was younger than me. I just knew that I wanted to have you. That was what was important for me." She hesitated.

"There was war coming and everything was dreadfully uncertain. I have written all this down." She shrugged dismissively. "Poems and things. They are not very good, but one day they may help you understand some of what went on." She took a reflective drag on her cigarette. "I just want you to know that it was only you I wanted out of all this." Her voice tailed off into a whisper, aware that she was repeating herself.

I could not find the words to respond, and I was confused by her vulnerability. It was only later, after I became a parent myself, that I began to understand how it must have been for her to have borne a child in those circumstances, with the German invasion gathering just across the Channel.

"He didn't want to marry me, and in any case, I wouldn't have wanted to get married just for the sake of it. Could you picture me married to a man like Uncle George or any of the other uncles?" That was a fair point. The thought of her being married to George or any of the others was laughable. I couldn't think of any man I knew as being a likely candidate for the role of her husband and my father. Anyway, no mortal could replace that mythical heroic father I had fashioned in my imagination.

She waited anxiously for some reaction. Having been hurt by the father, perhaps she was preparing herself to be judged by the son. I was too introspective and self-centred to worry about what she was thinking. I waited quietly for anger in me to boil up but it never quite came. Instead, I blinked back a few tears of self-pity and changed the subject.

"How do we get his details for this form?" I simply did not have the maturity to allow her the opportunity to explain or elaborate.

"Shaw has all that information. He's still in touch with your father so could arrange a meeting if you wanted that." Shaw again. I was grateful for all he had done for us but I was beginning to resent his continuing presence in our lives. I did not want him involved in all this.

"It's only dates and things. Perhaps Shaw can get Phyllis to add them to the form," I said. Phyllis Oliver, as Shaw's secretary, was the keeper of the many secrets surrounding Red Hill.

"I don't think Phyllis knows anything about this. Shaw is the only one who knows. That was what was agreed when your father left. Shaw can complete the form for you." There was an uncomfortable silence between us. "Morris got married after he left here. I think they've had a child. He is still teaching somewhere." She spoke carefully. "You haven't said if you want Shaw to fix up a meeting with him." I was too preoccupied to reply immediately. I couldn't think of him as 'Dad' or even 'my father'. Strangely, I was trying to say his name in my head to see what it sounded like before I actually spoke it. Morris was not a very heroic name. I didn't think I had heard of anyone called that.

"There wouldn't be any point in getting Shaw involved. Morris means nothing to me," I said finally. It was she who was the one who was important to me. She offered me strength, support and love, not my father. I never did find the words to tell her so. Inadvertently, with adolescent disregard for anyone but myself, I denied her the one opportunity she had ever had to talk about what really went on between her and my father. Neither did she have the opportunity to elaborate on the lie that had been constructed around my father and the cost to her of preserving the myth of him as the quiet hero.

Our uneasy conversation drew to a conclusion. I had to accept that the voracious bureaucracy needed to be fed. I agreed to Shaw filling in the blanks so that my passport could be processed.

While the shift to the Upper Cottage had given me some space to grow, it moved Mum away from the centre of things at Red Hill. She managed this well enough when I was away at school and only home during the holidays. However, with the prospect of me finishing school to find a job somewhere, we would have to learn to live together. Until then, her room at the school and then the cottage had been open house for any boy who wanted a smoke and a chat. Sometimes those chats would go on for hours and I found myself seething with resentment at the time she gave to others. Worst of all, I did not see the onset of loneliness in her, as the life she had been used to for twenty-five years was slowly changing. I have described our relationship as sometimes resembling that of an old married couple. Like an old married couple, we still laughed at the same things and chatted about the affairs of the day, but we avoided any contentious personal issues. Unlike an old married couple, we had never lived together before and had no history on which to establish a relationship that would work as we both grew older. Like any teenager, I was self-focused and intolerant of the older generation.

We never spoke of my father again. In my mother, I had the best possible model and teacher for just getting on with things. It would be many years before I would be ready to look for my father and attempt to make some sense of the fiction that had been created around my birth.

11

GROWING UP

My last school report from the Blue Coat finishes with *'We are looking forward to seeing him back in the 6th Form'.* It did not happen. School Certificate didn't prove quite the hurdle that the eleven and thirteen plus exams had been. I knew that staying on at school for another two years for A levels and then possibly university would cause money problems for Mum. There was another reason. In spite of, or perhaps because of, my Red Hill upbringing and Mum's own adventurous life, I was growing into a risk-averse young man. I wasn't prepared to be found wanting at university. I started to scan *The Times Literary Supplement* for suitable jobs that did not require strength in maths. Mum seemed keen to see me into safe work, preferably with some status.

Shaw was on the Library Committee of the Kent County Library. As 1957 was a time of full employment and with Shaw as a referee, my appointment as a library assistant at Kent County Library was pretty much assured. The interview was not particularly rigorous, and I was able to impress the interview panel with literary knowledge so recently developed at Liverpool. Mum was very pleased to see me into a stable job that, she felt, had some status and had the added bonus of being the source of a steady supply of new books for her to read. The library was only six miles away in Maidstone so I could easily get there on my bike or by bus.

It seemed to me that in 1957 everyone was having sex. Everyone except me. I was seventeen, starting my first job, and my only experience with girls was hurling provocative comments across to them in Mystery Park in Liverpool. For all the freedoms of my Red Hill upbringing, I was emerging as a naïve young man.

Mr Gen, the barber in the village, worked Brylcreem into my thick black hair, making it slick and greasy. He leaned forward as he combed the back into the imitation of a duck's arse. I was looking for a restrained Elvis style. This was right at the edge of Mr Gen's range, but he knew the days of a 'short back and sides' were gone. I could smell the tobacco on his breath as he worked with the comb and scissors, finishing off the job.

"First job eh? Buggered if I know what a librarian does." That made two of us, but at least I knew you didn't need School Cert maths for the job. He leaned closer to me and dropped his voice.

"You might be needing some…" he hesitated, searching for an adequate euphemism, "yer know what. Now you're starting work." I had no idea what he was talking about. I just grinned vacantly at the twin reflection of us in his mirror, waiting for some further explanation. He held another mirror so that I could see the result of his labours. This gave me a side-on view of myself, which is what I supposed others saw when they looked at me. Still more boy than man than I would have liked. Girls my age just seemed so much more experienced than me. The face that gazed back at me was hardly that of a man.

His work finished, Mr Gen flicked at my shoulders with his little brush. He looked around. There were no other customers waiting.

"Are you sure you don't want any? I got gossamer or standard. Most young fellas prefer the gossamer." This time he jerked his head towards the little glass cabinet alongside the mirror, and I was finally able to work out what I was being offered. It was then, in an act of bravado rather than intent, I bought my first packet of condoms. They looked and smelt like something out of my John Bull bike tyre puncture outfit.

The hierarchy of the library reflected the times. Everyone remotely identified as senior was called by his or her surname with the gender prefix, usually Miss. The rest of us were called by our Christian names. On my first day, I was greeted enthusiastically by Miss Wells, who was to be my manager. She had a habit of talking rather loudly as if addressing a meeting rather than an individual. She had wild grey hair tied in a bun and usually wore a high-necked blouse with a brooch at the throat. This, together with the grey skirt and sensible brown shoes, made her very much the stereotype of a librarian of the time.

Miss Wells introduced me to my new colleagues at morning tea. "This is Peter, girls. It will be good to have a man around to keep you all in order." Miss Wells smiled at her own little joke. I looked around me, alarmed and excited in equal measure. It seemed as though I was the only male in the place. Apart from Miss Wells's loyal assistant, Ursula, they were all young women about my age.

Librarianship, for me, turned out to be making tea, putting plastic jackets on books and making parcels to be sent to remote parts of the county. The attitude of the others to a male on their territory was generally welcoming. Judith, the love goddess with the long legs and the blonde hair to match, was an exception. She was completely indifferent to my presence; she was used to having hot adolescent eyes sweep across her body. She even encouraged it, smiling dreamily as she hitched up her tiny skirt prior to planting her pert little bottom onto the high stool we used when sitting at the catalogue. That is as far as it went, however. She made it very plain that work was something she fitted in between social engagements involving older men at the top end of county society. There always seemed to be sports cars with confident twenty year old men at the wheel waiting to pick her up from work. There was no place for a pimply-faced library assistant with that lot, although I did purchase a replica university scarf and flat hat just in case I got the call. I even considered taking up pipe smoking. Judith lighting a cigarette is an erotic fantasy that still, very occasionally, leaps into focus in the memorabilia of my mind.

My new colleagues did not seem to resent the fact that I was paid more than them for doing exactly the same work. This was based solely on gender rather than any elementary library skills that, in my case, were non-existent. The library was part of a larger site that encompassed the whole of the Kent County Council operation. Most of the staff there, at least the ones I had anything to do with, were young men about my age. There was lots of nudging and winking when I went over to the main building.

"Here he is then. Surprised he's got the energy to walk over here after what he's been getting up to with them library birds. Hanging out for it, they tell me."

I found that a self-satisfied smirk was the best response to that sort of ribbing. It brought me a completely unjustified reputation as a Lothario. The reality was quite different. Having spent my entire seventeen years in overwhelmingly male institutions, I wasn't quite sure how to manage in this new and tantalising environment.

Miss Wells looked after the morals of the borrowers diligently. It was she who decided what books were considered unsuitable for the open shelves or the book vans. How she came to such decisions was a mystery to the rest of us, but once she wrote 'sticky' on the library card, the book would be consigned to the warehouse in town, only to be retrieved if a borrower was bold enough to request it specifically.

After a few months she took me to one side. "I think you are ready for a change, Peter," she said, quietly for her. "I would like you to take charge of Wren's Cross." This was the warehouse on the other side of town where older books were retired to see out their days. It was also where sticky books were hidden away from prying eyes. "You'll ensure that everything is neat and tidy down there and the sticky books are stacked away each week."

I didn't know what I had done to earn such responsibility, but I suspected it was more a decision relating to gender than any particular ability. The prevailing philosophy was based on the notion that there was no point in giving girls opportunities to develop their careers as they were only going to get married and have babies. Women managers, like Miss Wells, frequently did more than most to preserve the status quo. I had already seen what it took to qualify as a librarian and I knew I wouldn't be staying around too long.

The Wren's Cross warehouse was an Aladdin's cave of erotica. In the fiction department, Henry Miller and Anais Nin were obvious candidates for the dungeons, where they jostled for space with less famous works that may have offended Miss Wells. The non-fiction area was much more interesting for me. There, the Dewey decimal catalogue system conveniently arranged a complete sexual lexicon in precise numerical order. So, 612.6 was where the medical material was located. There was also some riveting information to be found in the 613.96 and 392.6 sections. *The Kama Sutra*, Havelock Ellis, Freud and Kinsey all had numbers assigned, although I was never quite sure how the cataloguers worked out exactly which numbers fitted which particular sexual proclivity. The nude photograph section in the 770s was also rich material. These books had been ruled sticky for their own protection. Apparently, some borrowers couldn't resist scribbling enhancements or exclamation marks in inappropriate places.

For all the information at my disposal, I could find no advice on what exactly I was supposed to do with Mr Gen's condoms. It wasn't something I could ask Mr Gen about, and judging from their stories, mates in the village football team were well ahead of me in that department. I knew which part of my body the condom was supposed to cover, but I was not quite sure when or how coverage could be achieved. I had some vague idea that you put it on before going out, but there were some basic difficulties with the hydraulics when I tried that. Obtaining an erection was not the problem; I found the smell of my John Bull puncture outfit had a debilitating effect on that part of my anatomy. Freud, Kinsey and co did not have the answer to my difficulty, although one or two had quite scary references to what they called erectile dysfunction. There was even a whole book on that subject. So each week the theoretical side of my sexual education was completed at the warehouse in town, but I was far from passing, or even sitting, any practical examination in the subject.

It took me some time to stumble upon the revelation that the women around me were not, after all, a different species. And relationships with them were not always about sex. Although my testosterone-filled body, fanned by an oversupply of information coming from the sticky books and mates in the village football team, was telling me a different story. Friendships formed with one or two young women from that time have remained with me ever since.

At Red Hill it was possible to combine sporting interests like football with more aesthetic pursuits such as theatre and acting. This combination was a difficult concept for the rest of the village football team to understand. I remember having a particularly complicated situation to explain to my team mates when I was asked to take the only male role in the local Women's Institute drama production, which was scheduled for showing in a competition at the theatre in Maidstone. The play did quite well, and there was a small but favourable review of my performance in the local paper, which caused considerable mirth in the football club dressing room. I gave up acting after that. There was only so much piss-taking I could sustain in the pursuit of my art. In any case, I found, as I grew older, I became increasingly uneasy on stage. Self-consciousness is probably a fatal shortcoming in any aspiring actor.

Brenda Kemp started at the library at about the same time as I did. There was an innocence and sense of fun about her. She lacked the disconcerting knowingness of some of the others, was interested in me and, best of all, she was between boyfriends. Shared confidences in the plastic-jacketing room led to some experimentation around the parks of Maidstone and visits to our respective parents. If she was surprised about what went on at Red Hill, she did not show it.

Mum seemed to approve of Brenda and developed a warm relationship with her. Brenda's mother had died ten years previously. After that, her dad took her and her sister off to South Africa in a courageous, if ill-advised sea trip in a converted navy motor torpedo boat. In South Africa, there had been a string of sleep-in housekeepers who Brenda was required to call 'Auntie'. After a year or so of living on his wits, her dad had to accept that his attempts to settle in Durban had failed miserably. Red Cross intervention was required to get them back home. All these experiences seem to have exhausted her dad because, by the time I met him, he seemed a defeated man, married to a much younger and challenging woman. He was interested only in various moneymaking schemes of dubious merit and legality. Brenda worshipped him, but his clear priorities were his young wife and whatever scheme was currently on the go. Brenda had warned me there was tension between her and her stepmother. It seemed to me a quite different household from the Carters' in Crossmead, but I didn't have any experience of what living in a conventional household was all about or whether such a thing existed.

Brenda and I soon became an established boyfriend/girlfriend. We were inexperienced in the ways of the world, or the flesh. But we were very happy to discover these things together and embark upon a path that, in those days, would lead to a twelve month engagement and marriage. After that, well who knew? Neither of us knew much about family life.

Mum seemed happy that I was in a settled relationship with Brenda and had what she saw as a good job with some status. I lived at home with her in the cottage, but by then, I only ever went into the main building at Red Hill to have a bath. A new generation of Red Hill boys was coming through and many would not have known of my existence. MOF still remained at the centre of things at the school, and boys would still seek her out for a smoke and a chat. But there was something going seriously wrong that even I could not fail to notice.

Wednesday was still her half-day off. She went into Maidstone as we had always done. Stooped down with her bag of supplies from Sainsbury's, she would trudge down the hill from the bus stop past the oast houses and into the school drive. We developed an unspoken tradition on Wednesdays. In her bag of groceries there would be some treat for me. Sometimes it would be a special cheese to try. If the budget was underspent at Sainsbury's, there might be some clothing for me, perhaps a tie, selected with her unerring if conservative good taste. For my Wednesday contribution, I would always ensure that I used my privileged borrower status to bring home a selection of new books for her to browse through. Always there was a glass or two of sherry as we comfortably traversed the safe world of politics, Red Hill gossip and what was going on with my job. One Wednesday I found her sitting in her chair, the shopping scattered around her and a sherry glass in her hand.

"Hello, Mum. What's happened here?" I said, nodding towards the shopping bags and their spilled contents.

"Oh those. I was just going to unpack them." She struggled to frame her words. "What's in the book bag?" she asked.

I did not recognise the diversion for what it was. "I've left it on the table. Go on and have a look while I unpack the shopping."

She levered herself from her chair and walked unsteadily to the table. She held a book in her hands, moving it back and forth, trying to focus on the title page. I looked at the sherry bottle. She had obviously drunk too much, but not in a way we could acknowledge and joke about. She looked up from the pile of books on the table. Her eyes were damp and uncomprehending. I looked away uncomfortably, not knowing how to react. We had been through so much, and she had always been there, strong and resilient. Yet suddenly there was a bleakness and vulnerability about her that I had never seen before.

"I'll just pack these things in the cupboard downstairs," I said, picking up the tins and other bits of shopping. "Then I think I'll go off to bed."

In the spilled shopping there was a separate package from Laveys, the man's shop in town. My treat for that week was a tasteful blue-striped tie.

I did not want to engage her in conversation, because I knew she would struggle to respond. That would be embarrassing for both of us. "Thanks for the tie Mum," I whispered, kissing her warm cheek goodnight. She smiled weakly but said nothing.

Lying in bed, I could hear her moving about in the next room. The next day she was up early as she always was. The flat was immaculate, and there was no sign of the sherry bottle. Much to my relief she said nothing about what had gone on the night before. If I had been a more aware young man, I might have given some thought to the fact that the time was fast approaching when she would no longer be at the centre of things at Red Hill. I might have realised that, unless one of the boys came to see her in the evening, she was reliant almost entirely upon me for company. She was perceptive enough to know that I would be leaving home soon and would be unselfish enough to encourage me to do so. I might have even realised that, isolated from her diminishing family circle and with few friends outside Red Hill, loneliness was stalking her. I was not an aware young man. I just thought she was worrying about money again.

For six days a week, everything remained fine between us, but I came to dread coming home on Wednesdays and finding her in various states of distress, depending on how empty the sherry bottle was. I was unwilling to confront her. She had always been the strong one and I simply did not have the skills to manage a confrontation. Neither was there anyone I could talk to without humiliating her further. So Wednesdays, which hitherto had been an oasis of quiet pleasure we had often enjoyed together, became the day of the week that was clouded with despair and tension. Nothing of this ever seeped outside the two of us to the wider community of Red Hill or anywhere else. It was my turn to guard a secret.

12

BRANCHING OUT

At last it was time for me to take a small risk. For the first time I stepped outside Shaw's protection. I was nineteen when I applied to join the Civil Service, knowing that it would mean a move to London or, with any luck, further afield. The application form invited successful candidates to nominate their three preferences for postings. I proudly showed Mum my nominations. Graham Greene had not been wasted on me. The Foreign Office was Number 1, the Colonial Office was Number 2 with the Home Office as a very distant Number 3, more to make up the numbers than anything else. Although Harold Macmillan's 'wind of change' was gathering momentum, British red was still spread like a stain over the map of the world. I would be happy to serve the Empire in some foreign land.

A letter arrived with the Civil Service crest. Mum sat opposite me while I tore open the envelope. I was told I had been appointed to a position as clerical officer by HM Prison Commissioners, then a part of the Home Office. I was to report for duty at HM Prison Holloway in North London. Carrying the white man's burden would have to wait. Nominating the Home Office just to make up the numbers had obviously been a mistake.

"That'll be interesting," Mum said without irony when I read out the contents of the letter. All I knew about Holloway Prison was that it was the largest women's prison in the country. I did not know that it was there, just a few years previously, that Ruth Ellis had been the last woman hanged for murder.

In those days hostel accommodation was available for out-of-town civil servants. Mine was in an eight-storey Lancaster Gate converted mansion, near Hyde Park. I soon found out why it was so cheap. I was sharing a room with two others, something I had got used to at my various schools, so it was not a hardship. There was a wash handbasin in the corner, but there was a bit of a walk around landings and staircases to get to the toilets and bathroom. There was the familiar institutional smell of cabbage and polish. Food was supplied as part of the rent, which was just as well as money would always run out towards the end of the month. It was a sociable place. We were all in new jobs, broke and excited about being in London on our own. Better still, there was the girls' lodgings a few doors down the road. Brenda had also moved to London, so we now had to manage our relationship through the minefield of temptation that London represented.

I tried to get home to Mum at Red Hill every other weekend, but this began to stretch out to once a month as my social life became increasingly crowded. Furthermore, in winter, the hostel football team had a busy fixture list at the weekend that, to me, seemed more important than visits home.

It was a drizzly north London day when I reported for duty on my first day in the Civil Service. The Holloway Prison building squatted, dark and impassive, across a long cobbled courtyard off the Camden Road in Islington. High smoke-blackened brick walls ran to the left and to the right of an imposing studded door, in which was set a smaller door with a grille. The huge metal knocker was slippery and cold as I swung it against the striker. A hollow sound rang out and after a few seconds a face appeared at the metal grille built inside the door. Thick eyebrows met across a wide nose. The eyes narrowed as he squinted towards me.

"Yes?" he asked.

"Peter Farrell. I'm due to start work here." I rummaged in my bag and took out the letter of appointment I had received and waved it in front of the grille.

"Hang on a minute, boy." There was a Welsh lilt about the voice. After some rattling of keys, the smaller door swung open. "Follow me," he said as he walked into a cluttered room marked 'Gatehouse'. A cigarette was held in his cupped hand so he did not offer to shake mine. I waited while he rested his cigarette on the ashtray and reached for the clipboard on the desk. "Oh yeah. Here we are, then," he said, leaning over towards the phone. "I'll get someone down from the Steward's Office. You'll be working in the Discipline Office."

I didn't like the sound of that at all. "Are you sure that's right?" I pulled out the Prison Commissioners' letter. "It says here I am a clerical officer and I will be employed by the Governor."

He stopped dialling, put down the phone, sighed theatrically and turned to me. "Dr Taylor's the Governor here boyo. I don't think she is going to want to bother with a little twat like you. Mr Egerton, the Steward, is in charge of the Discipline Office where most of the clerks work. Now, if you don't mind," he said heavily, "I'll give 'im a ring."

There was nothing that I had experienced in my life to date that could have prepared me for seeing the inside of Holloway Prison for the first time. This was a world that lived entirely within the dark, sooty walls that encircled it. A young woman prison officer escorted me across a courtyard. We were making for some flagstone steps that led into the main building. We prepared to skirt around a work group of twenty or so prisoners who were brushing, disconsolately and without much impact, the cobblestone ground. They wore drab dresses, buttoned down the front. Some of the younger ones had hitched their dresses up an inch or two. Some were wrapped in cardigans over their smock-like dresses. Most wore short grey socks with feet pushed into heavy black shoes. An older, grey-haired officer in a blue uniform was watching them with equal boredom, keys swinging at her waist.

They stopped what they were doing when they could see we were approaching.

"You're a man and you're new, so don't be surprised if we get a reaction." The prison officer moved a little closer to me. "Just look straight ahead and don't say nothing."

"Oooo, new meat! Bit young for you, ain't he miss?" I was taking the officer's advice and looking steadily ahead. The comments rained in on us. There was much laughter as they fed off one another.

"You looking for some older stuff boy? Have a look at this. I can show you a bit more if you come down to our wing later on." I didn't know what she was showing me as I determinedly held my eyes in front and kept my step measured.

Finally we reached the flagstones and moved into the main building. I was immediately aware of the sounds that echoed off the stone walls. Ordinary conversations seemed to be amplified as they were thrown against the high arched ceilings. There was the sound of clattering trolleys, keys smacking against bars and doors slamming. Somewhere in the distance someone was singing, or perhaps it was a scream. The smell of stale cooking fat from that morning's breakfast permeated the air, mingling with the familiar institutional smell of disinfectant.

To three hundred or so women and their captors, this grim noisy place was the real world. It was as if Islington, bustling just a few yards away over that high dark wall, did not exist. Each day I went to work and walked through the prison gate, leaving London behind and entering that other separate darker world that was just as real to those who inhabited it. I already had some experience of moving between two worlds and adjusting to the realities of others, so going to work at Holloway was not as difficult for me as it could have been.

'The Steward' was an archaic term for what was essentially the administration manager. Mr Egerton was a gentlemanly civil servant of the old school. Like Mr Egerton himself, his office was quietly comfortable and a complete contrast to the bleak surroundings in which it existed. Mr Egerton stood in his pinstripe suit fiddling nervously with his watch strap, trying to put his new staff member at ease. He spoke encouragingly about this being the first step for me.

"It's an unusual environment, but you will learn things here about the administration of government that you could not get in other departments." He made it sound as if I could look outside and see Whitehall and the Houses of Parliament when, in fact, his office overlooked one of the yards where remand prisoners wandered around aimlessly, smoking, as they saw out the endless days awaiting their call to court. Mr Egerton gave me a brief history of the place.

Like Colney Hatch, where Mum had lived and worked in the twenties, Holloway had been built by the Victorians, full of good Christian values based upon their view of humane imprisonment and rehabilitation. Unfortunately, these intentions foundered under the demands of a society bent on retribution for the smallest of crimes. Holloway Castle was originally built to hold male and female prisoners, but in 1902, twenty years after it opened, it became a women-only prison. The women imprisoned there were serving sentences ranging from a few days for unpaid fines to life for murder.

The quaintly named Discipline Office was simply an old prison term for the office that looked after inmate records. There was also an Accounts Office and a Stores Office. The interiors were more Bob Cratchit than Steve Jobs. Somewhere in the Prison Commission archives will be the Holloway Prison Reception Register with my careful joined-up writing making the entries for the day. There were a few of us younger staff in the office. The core group of the office staff were older men, although there were one or two women. Mostly this group fed happily off precedent, institutional knowledge and reactionary opposition to change of any sort. Once you were inside them, the offices could have been any Civil Service offices anywhere in the country, but I was reminded where I was every time I left the confines of the office. The prison wings fanned out from the centre where the Chief Officer and her senior staff were located. Each wing had three or four landings connected by steel staircases. Cells were dotted along each landing like a pigeon loft. Wire mesh was secured over the well between the two landings. That covered off one method of committing suicide.

I frequently visited the Chief's office so soon got accustomed to the noise, sense of claustrophobia and boredom that prevailed on the wings. Women in the drab prison dresses who were not employed in the jam factory, the laundry or other work parties were milling around smoking, talking or just staring. As a young man, nervously clutching whatever piece of paper that needed signing by the Chief, I was an easy target. I learned not to take shouted insults too seriously and resisted the temptation to respond in kind. If my brief presence released a little tension on the wing, then I was probably achieving more in those few minutes than I was in an eight-hour day in the office.

The introduction of the Street Offences Act of 1959, which specifically made it an offence for 'any common prostitute to loiter or solicit for the purpose of prostitution' had an immediate impact upon Holloway. Particular streets in west and east London were targeted by the police in a massive clean-up campaign. Offenders unable or unwilling to pay their fines ended up in Holloway. Market forces then came into play. The employer of a woman locked up for prostitution would calculate at what point it would be economic to pay the balance of the fine in order to get her back to work. Typically, there would be a call from the gatehouse that went something like this:

"Got a Mr Mancini here. Wants to pay the fine for Muriel O'Donnell."

"The balance for release today will be three pounds, fourteen and sixpence."

"He says okay."

I would then go down to the gatehouse, take the cash from Mr Mancini and hand him a Prison Commissioners' receipt. He would then wait for Muriel O'Donnell to be brought up.

The whole scenario would be repeated during the next few weeks, with a different cast of players or, sometimes, the same players using different names.

During my time at Holloway there was a change of governor when the long serving Lady (Dr) Taylor moved to the Commissioners' Office and was replaced by Joanna Kelley. I was far too low in the hierarchy to have anything to do with either of them. Both seem to have been genuinely admired for the work they did at Holloway under the impossibly difficult circumstances that existed there.

In his efforts to familiarise me with Holloway, Mr Egerton had dutifully spoken of the rehabilitation and education programmes being run. Yet from my perspective, it soon became apparent that whatever the Governor may have wished, the first priority of the prison officers was to contain and control those sent to the prison by the courts; I was to be a very small and compliant administrative cog in that mechanism.

Since Ruth Ellis was hanged at Holloway in 1955, there had been some limitations placed on the death penalty, but it had not been completely erased from the statute books. There were even formal instructions in the Prison Manual covering all the minute details about how such an event would be managed. I once read these instructions through and realised, for the first time, what serving the Crown could mean whether you were the Governor, a prison officer or merely the minion required to supply the paraphernalia of an execution. At nineteen, I hadn't developed my mother's perception and courage to question hierarchies, and it was a bit early in my career to be confronted with such a fundamental issue of principle. I resolved to leave the job rather than have any part, however miniscule, in an execution, should that situation ever arise. Fortunately my resolution was never tested. There were to be no more executions at Holloway.

Brenda and I were still boyfriend and girlfriend although it was inhibiting for us both as we were tempted by a freer life in London. We were products of our respective upbringings, both looking for stability, which meant marriage rather than just living together. Sooner or later we would have to take the next step or finish the relationship altogether. There was a happy inevitability about our engagement and marriage twelve months later. Brenda was the only person I knew who had any understanding at all about what it meant to be brought up outside a conventional family. The word 'conventional' became important to us as we happily planned our life together. There was a mutual need there, but our love for one another was no less because of that. We were set on a conventional path that would lead to marriage, mortgage and children. Somewhere, there may have been the sound of a door closing softly on a youth that, in my case, could have been more misspent.

'Being engaged' for twelve months before marriage was a state neither of us was particularly comfortable with, but that tended to be the norm before the sixties began to swing. As part of our plan for the future, I volunteered to be a foundation staff member at a new psychiatric prison that was being constructed at Grendon Underwood, just outside Aylesbury. So in 1962, the move to Grendon Prison was all to do with getting a house with the job rather than any particular commitment to penal reform that Grendon was later to represent. Subsidised prison housing was to be available to staff as an incentive to live in such a remote area. We were doing everything we could to create a normal environment around ourselves. We would have a brand new house waiting for us when we returned from our honeymoon. And apart from my time boarding at the Carters, I had never lived in a house before.

Our wedding in Headcorn Church was all we wished for. I look at those wedding photos now and see the bride, stunning in white, and me in my uncomfortable blue suit but measuring up well as the bridegroom. We proudly paid for our own reception in the Oddfellows Hall. As those occasions often are, it was an uneasy mix of families and friends who had little in common, but we were happy. None of Mum's sisters turned up, but she seemed to cope well without them. I watched her circulating in those unfamiliar surroundings. It was a long time since she had attended a social gathering outside Red Hill. Shaw was present but sat quietly in the background with his wife Joan. Brenda's dad got us a deal on the champagne that we paid for on a sale or return basis. We never did see the refunds on the full bottles that were returned.

The reception over and the speeches made, Brenda and I caught the train from Headcorn. The ticket collector smiled indulgently as he locked us in our own compartment. I looked out at Mum on the platform, standing in front of the small group seeing us off. She had a faint smile on her face. She never wanted me to take the risks that she had. I was now married and in a good job in the Civil Service, so I had achieved what she sought for me. She would have known my focus would be elsewhere in the years ahead and would deal with that in her own way. I turned towards Brenda as the train gathered speed for London.

13

A BEGINNING AND AN END

Brenda and I moved into our new house in Spring Hill Road on the Grendon Prison estate. We had no furniture, but as we looked out from the bedroom window across the rolling Buckinghamshire farmland, we felt sure of the future and ourselves. I was once again back in the countryside and living in the confines of an institution miles from anywhere.

Locals in Grendon Underwood and the immediate neighbourhood did not seem to resent the development of another prison in the area, although there must have been some apprehension, given the type of inmate who was going to end up there.

Springhill House had been built as a country residence in 1872, and it still retained its ivy-covered protection against the world. It seems to have had a chequered history since then, including being a wartime base for the Secret Service. In 1953, it opened as one of the early so-called open prisons in the country. Grendon Psychiatric Prison was established on land behind Springhill, but it was to be quite a different institution from Springhill or any other prison in the country for that matter. Dr W. J. Gray, a quietly assertive Scot, was to be the man in charge. There were two things immediately apparent to outsiders. Dr Gray was a psychiatrist, and his title was Medical Superintendent, not Governor.

After a few days working there, and before the inmates began to arrive, it became apparent to me that this was not going to be a typical prison in the Holloway mould. Dr Gray was preparing to receive the most difficult of male prisoners. The type of offending was no bar to being accepted at Grendon. Deeply disturbed inmates, including diagnosed psychopaths, would be accepted there. Gray was determined Grendon would not become a dumping ground within the prison system, and to that end, there would be some vetting of inmates before he or his senior staff would accept a transfer. The vetting would involve some assessment of the willingness and ability of the inmate to participate in the therapeutic community that was to be the cornerstone of the approach at Grendon. Dr Gray was proposing to develop a more democratic regime. This was going to be done without compromising the basic requirement to ensure the protection of society from its two hundred and fifty or so inmates, which included some of the most dangerous offenders in custody anywhere in the country.

The facilities may have been sparkling new, but the high perimeter wall was as uncompromising as any maximum security prison anywhere. Inside the wall there were green spaces rather than flagstones. The accommodation blocks were hospital-like, but once inmates started to arrive, the cacophony of sounds and the prison smells soon took the sparkle out of the environment.

Most of the staff assigned to Grendon volunteered to transfer there from other prisons around the country. A high proportion of the volunteers were specialist hospital officers. Under Gray's leadership there was less reliance upon hierarchy to enforce compliance between officers and inmates or between officers themselves. Civilian staff were accepted as valid contributors to the prison community and there was an opportunity for us to participate in some of the group activities. Some of the staff used to the 'control and contain' philosophy of traditional secure prisons did not adjust easily to a more consultative regime. Some staff were very critical of group therapy meetings, library committees, sports committees and the array of other groups designed to involve inmates in taking some responsibility. A dismissive acronym – MFM for More Fucking Meetings – gained currency for a while, but most staff supported what was being tried, so far as they understood it. Inevitably there were some spectacular failures that would delight the cynics amongst the officers as they piled in with batons to subdue some disturbance or other.

I did not fully comprehend what a ground-breaking institution I had stumbled upon, but I was familiar with some of the language and philosophy. One day I was working with an inmate doing a storeroom stocktake. Brian had been selected to work with me as he was brilliant with figures; this may have contributed to his offending. We had been working together off and on for a few weeks.

"Christ, Pete, I've gotta get out of here," he suddenly said anxiously.

"Sorry, Brian." I smiled and was about to give some throwaway comment that only the Parole Board could get him out when I noticed he was looking at the clock.

"I've gotta group therapy session with the new psych. I'll be in the shit if I'm late." I had never seen him like this before.

"Don't worry Brian, I'll ring and tell them you are on your way and they can send someone to escort you over," I said, reaching for the phone.

It was only a few years previously when a Red Hill boy would suddenly leave a game of cards or whatever it was that we were playing because "I've got to go to analysis with Shaw."

I might not have fully understood the scope of the Grendon regime, but I was familiar with the language and practices of a therapeutic community. I began to feel comfortable at work for the first time.

Things were also comfortable and happy at home. Brenda had a job in Aylesbury, so I usually arrived home first. The house was empty in every sense. We had a bed, with a couple of chairs sitting in the lounge trying to look bigger than they were. We got an extra bed in for Mum when she came up to stay for her first visit. The last time she had travelled north of London was when she and I went to Liverpool. She stayed with us at Grendon for two days. There was a strange uneasiness about her in the unfamiliar environment she found herself in. She liked Brenda, was pleased for us and very interested in how my job was going, but there was something indefinable happening. It was as if she was unsure how a mother-in-law should behave. That was not surprising. Brenda and I felt we were still learning about what was expected of us as husband and wife. When it was time for Mum to go, I walked with her down to the bus stop. We talked easily about inconsequential things, just as we used to when I was little and we walked up to the bus stop on her days off.

"Bye, Mum," I said kissing her as the Aylesbury bus arrived. "See you soon. Perhaps we'll get down to Red Hill."

"No, you've got your life here," she smiled. "You need to get settled in before you think about coming down to see me." She squeezed my hand briefly and climbed onto the bus.

Living on a new prison housing estate where the landlord and employer were the same brought problems of its own, particularly as we had no children. Joining in was important, so we made sure that one or other of us was seen at the various committees and clubs that had sprung up on the estate. I took up football refereeing and used to stoically pedal my bike to football fixtures in villages all over Buckinghamshire every Saturday. This at least took me away from the prison estate for a few hours. Refereeing village games, some of which had a long history of ferocious rivalry dating back to the Black Plague, was not a place to assimilate myself into country life outside the prison. Brenda also tried to look elsewhere, but she was simply too young for the Women's Institute activities in the local village.

We never had unexpected visitors at night, so when there was a banging on the door one night, I leapt out of bed and fiddled around on the floor for some clothes.

"Must be a problem up at the prison," I said, more to myself than Brenda, who was emerging from a deep sleep. I didn't usually get called out for that sort of thing.

"Be careful, love. You don't know who that is down there," Brenda warned. She was suddenly wide awake. It was a good thought to have. There had been no escapes from Grendon in the twelve months since it had opened, but there was always that possibility. Pulling on some clothes and clattering down the stairs, breath steaming against the cold, I took a broom handle from the cupboard in the hall, just in case. I needn't have worried. I could see the blue prison officer uniform through the mottled glass in the door.

It was one of the older officers who I didn't know very well. He was stamping up and down to keep his circulation going. "There was a phone call for you a couple of hours ago. Here's the name and number you're to ring." He pushed the piece of paper into my hand. "Stan's on night shift. He said to go up to the prison and use the phone there. It sounded urgent."

I opened the note. The caller was Shaw, but the number I had to ring was not his. My mouth dried, and I felt my stomach lurch. Shaw would only be ringing about one person, and it would be bad news.

I called up the stairs to Brenda. "There's been a call from Shaw. He wants me to ring him. I'll have to go up to the prison and ring from there. Sounds like we'll have to go down to Kent."

The walk from the staff housing settlement to the prison itself was pleasant enough in normal circumstances. That night, as I leant into the sharp wind of early winter, I was not aware of the neat new terraced staff houses, nor the grounds of Springhill House that I had to pass through before I got to the main prison building. My torch picked out the sign – *HM Prison Grendon Underwood. Only authorised visitors beyond this point.*

I reflected upon Mum's recent visit and the uncertainties that surrounded it. I remembered her insistence that we should concentrate on our lives and not worry about visiting her. I had written to her every week, just as I had when I was away at school, but we had never really talked since she told me about my father. Now this.

The wall loomed above me. There was a small entry gate set into the huge studded door. I rang the bell and heard it reverberating inside.

The spyhole cover was pulled back cautiously. Fortunately, it was a face I knew.

"Hi Stan. Just come up to use the phone."

"How long you been married and already you're up here ringing up your bit on the side in the middle of the night? Dunno about you young buggers," he said, pulling the gate wider to let me in. I couldn't give him the response he wanted and just pushed on into the gate office where the phone was. The number Shaw gave was not his but the number for the Royal West Kent Hospital in Maidstone. My hand shook as I dialled the number.

"Mrs Farrell has had a stroke. She was found on the road below the school." My immediate thought was she would have been going to the pub for a bottle of sherry. She always drank alone at home. That was part of the problem. I was later to find out that I was wrong. She had been on her way to meet some friends at the pub. The voice on the phone was gentle, well versed in giving news in the middle of the night of lives damaged. I didn't know what a 'stroke' was, but it sounded serious. "At this stage, she is in a very critical condition. Mr Otto Shaw said you are the next of kin. Is that right?"

'Yes." I wondered vaguely if my father would count as next of kin but I could not deal with those complications then. "I'll come straight away."

Brenda had already packed a suitcase and checked when the trains with connections to Maidstone left from Aylesbury.

"I've got Freddie Lane's taxi on standby to take us to Aylesbury. He said we can pay him later," she said.

We carefully avoided talking about what might be waiting for us at the hospital, preferring to concentrate upon the logistics of the four-hour journey. Mum didn't die that night. I didn't recognise her. She was already withdrawing from the battling, resilient person I knew. Her face was pasty and sunken without her teeth. Her grey hair was spread loosely across the pillow. Saliva dribbled from the side of her mouth. I leant towards her and wiped her chin, shocked at her helplessness. The nurses spoke to her in the condescending tones of the kindergarten. She would have hated that. When she opened her eyes they were lifeless, although I thought I saw a brief flicker of recognition. She moved her head slightly, her mouth working, as if trying to speak. No sound came out.

"How are we today my dear? Ooh look! You got a little bruise when you fell. I'll make that better for you." I could not identify the nurses as people; there was the fat one, the thin one, the pretty one and the one with spots. This one was the thin one. "You're a lucky girl. Look, your lovely son has come to visit you. He's been here every day." She fussed around the bed. "The doctor will be along soon," she said to me as if to announce the relief of Mafeking. The doctor never did appear. I had no idea that it was quite possible Mum could understand everything I was saying to her. I found the courage to whisper soliloquies to her while she lay unresponsive but breathing heavily.

Brenda and I stayed at the cottage at Red Hill. It seemed an empty place without Mum's presence.

I was just finding my feet in the adult world. It was only then, too late, that I could talk to her of love and understand what that meant for both of us. It was only then I appreciated the scope of her sacrifice as she sheltered me at Red Hill but still let me make my own way. On our visits to the hospital, I half expected her to sit up, put her teeth in, berate the nurses for their condescending manner and walk out of there. She never did. Just once during those last ten days she was in hospital did she manage to form some words. I could see the effort she was making and bent forward.

"Why didn't you tell me?" She whispered quite clearly into my ear. Her eyes closed and her right hand gripped mine tightly.

I would like to think that she had heard my belated words of love, but I'll never know. Her whispered question could just as easily have been words of admonition for Morris.

The next day when I visited, her bed was empty. Some nurses I didn't recognise were busily tidying things up for the next patient. I did not need them to tell me why Mum was no longer there, but neither did I understand that I could ask to see where she was. In those days funeral directors attended to the logistics of death. I thought it was my job to leave them to do that and to maintain a stoic face to the world. I went out into the lobby outside the hospital ward to give the news to Brenda and Phyllis who were waiting there. Phyllis drove us back to the cottage at Red Hill in her Morris Minor. None of us could trust ourselves to speak. I gripped a brown paper bag on my lap. I couldn't remember anyone giving it to me, but there it was. I opened it up and peered inside. It was her handbag and some of the other things she had on her when she was found. It was 15 September 1964. She was sixty-five years old when she died.

In the years that have followed her death, my greatest sadness has been that I was unable to have adult-to-adult conversations with her on a personal level. She had told me some stories, and I have found out so much more since she died, but I never really knew this woman who gave me so much.

It seemed like all of Red Hill had crowded into the church at East Sutton. I was not the only one left bereft and confused by MOF's death. Ted Brown, the gardener, sought me out before I went into the church. He looked uncomfortable in his rough brown suit. He held my gaze briefly. "She was one in a million, your mum. I remember when she arrived, before the war." His grey eyes blinked rapidly. "Dunno how we are going to manage without her," he said in his Kentish burr. He had lived in the area all his life and had been the gardener at Charlton Court before Shaw moved Red Hill there. Like Mum, Ted had been at Red Hill from the very beginning. "I have to go off now to ring the bell for her." Ted was a bell ringer at the church. Soon, there was the sound of a single bell echoing from the church tower.

Many others came up to me, but I was fighting to retain some composure and barely heard what was being said.

After the service Morley Gayton quietly appeared by my side. Morley, who taught history and geography, seems to have been regarded by many boys at Red Hill as the best teacher there. In a place where it was easy to get on the wrong side of people, Morley was universally liked and respected. His amiable and stable nature only collapsed around him when he was given out at cricket. It was a very brave umpire who would raise a finger to give an lbw decision against Morley. He was very patient with me when I went to him for extra geography lessons while I was struggling at Eltham. It all made sense when Morley explained it.

He waited for me to turn towards him. He seemed to have thought carefully, even rehearsed, what he wanted to say.

"It wasn't very easy for men to gain her friendship," he hesitated, his familiar bushy eyebrows knitted into a frown, "but *I* felt respect and friendship for *her*." He gripped my arm. "I admired her most as a mother faced with nearly every disadvantage but doing a perfect job." He turned quickly away and joined his family.

I swallowed deeply and moved towards the graveside, which was in the far corner of the graveyard by the hop field. The hop vines were full. Harvest would not be far away. Inconsequently, I wondered if Londoners still came down from the East End to pick the hops.

Three of the aunts, Agnes, Hilda and May, arrived from London to help us clear up the cottage after the funeral. They crowded in with Brenda and me at the tiny flat over the garage. The object of the exercise as they saw it was to clear up and get on with life. They had all turned up at Agnes's place when George had died a few years previously. That's how you dealt with death. Our family did not have a wake, we had a clear-up. The three sisters set about the clear-up with some energy. Laughingly, they tried on Mum's clothes and shared them amongst themselves or discarded them as the fancy took them. I felt Mum's presence gradually disappearing as they scrubbed and polished the flat in a whirlwind of genuine but, for me, misplaced kindness. When they talked about her, they spoke mainly about the fifteen year old they remembered rather than the complex person she had become. To them, she remained an enigma.

"I think you should see these, Peter." Agnes had a small box of papers in her hand. "There might be something about your dad there." They must have assumed that I had been told or found out about my father because nobody in Mum's family had ever mentioned him before in my presence. They were obviously more curious about him than I was. The papers were indeed about him but not quite what Agnes was expecting. They were the poems Mum had written just before I was born. I knew of their existence because she had told me about them when she told me about Morris. I was not ready to read them then.

Uncle Arthur came down in his Austin 7 to pick up his wife May and the other two sisters. They left for London, leaving Brenda and me to carry on with the clear-up which in fact turned into a clear-out. With Mum no longer there and me living away, the cottage would be required by Shaw for Red Hill. In the space of two weeks, all vestiges of Mum's presence and my childhood and youth had been removed.

Shaw kept away. I always respected but never quite understood Mum's unswerving loyalty to him. He was charming, charismatic, kind and had been a mentor for her. I knew from what Phyllis and others told me that he often acknowledged to them how pivotal Marion had been over the years and how reliant upon her he was. For all his considerable ability with words, I don't think he ever conveyed those thoughts to Mum directly. Instead, an antique pewter jug, a rare print or a book would occasionally be left for her in the linen room with a scribbled note from him. For me, the flat over the garage at Red Hill had been home. Shaw took his role as my legal guardian very seriously, in a remote Victorian sort of way. After the funeral, I went to see him. There was something I wanted to ask.

An extension had been built at Red Hill. It was an appalling piece of 1960s architecture quite out of keeping with the rest of what had been Charlton Court. Shaw had moved his study in there, but very little else had changed. Knocking on his study door, I remembered those dreadful farewell meetings with him at the end of the school holidays when I had to return to boarding school. Nothing had changed much in the study. There was still the rich smell of tobacco. Shaw fondled the leather pouch in that endless ritual of the pipe smoker. I knew to wait until the pipe had been filled, lit and drawn upon before the interview began.

"Terrible thing. Terrible. You know there's nothing in the will, don't you?" he said, leaning back, gazing reflectively at the smoke from his pipe, drifting upwards towards the yellowing ceiling. I waited for a belated tribute, but it did not come. On occasions like this, Shaw would normally be well in control and able to lead the dialogue. It was unusual to find him struggling for the right words to say. I hadn't come to talk about money. I knew that there would be no money, just as I knew there would be no debts.

"Does my father know about all this?" I couldn't frame the words 'my mother' or 'Mum' and 'death' in the same sentence. I realised Shaw would still be in touch with Morris.

He frowned at his pipe. "You don't need to worry about that. You won't be hearing anything from that source." He turned and looked at me blankly, hesitated, went to say something but decided against it. I had never seen him uncertain before. I allowed the silence to fill the space between us.

If my father still didn't want to know me, then stuff him. Although I was happily married to the woman I loved, I had never felt as alone as I did then. The lie surrounding my birth had lain undisturbed for seventeen years, until I had to fill in that passport application form in 1957. Seven years later, this could be my last opportunity to uncover what really happened and confront Shaw and perhaps my father as well, but too much time had passed. Nothing could assuage the pain Mum had unnecessarily undergone to protect me from the truth. It was she, rather than me, who had been damaged by the conspiracy. I reasoned my wounds were more superficial and would heal in time. There was nothing to be achieved by a confrontation then. In any case, I did not have the stomach for it.

Shaw seemed almost relieved when I stood to go.

14

ARRIVAL IN NEW ZEALAND

A few months after we got back from the funeral we had confirmation that Brenda was pregnant. We had, by this time, moved off the prison estate into a tiny house in Steeple Aston, a small Oxfordshire village not too far from Grendon. Nick's birth in Banbury Hospital was not easy. Back in 1965, husbands were not welcome at such events. Eventually as the labour went on and on, I was allowed to sit beside Brenda's bed. I missed Mum's presence with her simple pragmatism and wry humour. Later, I took my son, that tiny squalling dependent person, in my arms. There was love, and there was wonder. Brenda looked over at me. I nervously returned her smile. There were two of us. We were okay. We would manage.

I was still enjoying work at Grendon, but there was a restlessness about us that neither of us could pin down. When Mum died, I had lost my anchor and had become more attracted to risk as I wondered about the future. Brenda had finally reconciled herself to the fact that her dad was not going to change; the relationship she had with her stepmother remained poisonous. She had long ago lost any anchor she may have had, and she was always the greater risk taker of the two of us.

There were signs of a new hopeful era in the mid-sixties. The Tories under Sir Alec Douglas-Home had lost the election. Harold Wilson was there, leading Labour. Capital punishment had finally been removed from the books, and amazingly, West Ham United had won the FA Cup. My job was still interesting, Nick was doing well and, in another thirty years, our mortgage would be paid off. Perhaps this was not the time to be thinking about going to another country. We both had a sense that, if we were not careful, middle age might hit us prematurely. Having at last got ourselves on the first step on the ladder towards what we perceived to be conventional family life, we began to fantasise about living in more exotic places.

The whole concept may have remained a fantasy had I not seen that the Commonwealth Relations Office was advertising for administrative staff. Chances to serve the Crown in foreign postings and return a rich man were the shallow thoughts I had in mind when I applied. The interview in Whitehall went well enough. Three or four years in the Civil Service and I was becoming quite adept at such exchanges. I did note that at least one member of the interview panel had some concerns about the lack of a degree, or even A levels, in my educational qualifications. The absence of Latin in my O levels was also raised. It was made clear that, if I was considered for an overseas posting, it would be at a very junior level, and I could not expect to advance further without a degree.

While I was waiting for the Commonwealth Relations Office to make up its mind, the interview there had raised other options. I started to research the possibility of immigrating to New Zealand.

Brenda and I devoured the literature provided by the New Zealand High Commission for assisted immigrants. There was talk of hard work and hard play and Jack being as good as his master. The pictures showed contented men in double-breasted suits smoking pipes and women happily pushing prams. It seemed a beautiful place. The quiet smugness of the publicity material suited us, compared with the brashness of Australia or Canada. I did have some vague sense that Mum's anger about intellectual and social snobbery had been passed on to me and that

New Zealand offered a more egalitarian society. She must have had some small connection with New Zealand; why else would she have had the print of Eruera Patuone, Rangatira of the Ngāpuhi tribe, which she had hung in my room at Red Hill? How did she know who he was? I would like to say we had grander motives for wanting to move to New Zealand than just the need to break free from a predictable existence, but that simply was not so.

Thinking about going was one thing; getting the approval of the New Zealand Government to assist with the fares was quite another. The days of wholesale assisted immigration had passed except for those with particular skills or with an employer who would sponsor them. I wrote direct to the New Zealand Department of Justice in Wellington in an attempt to persuade them I had unique transferable skills as a prison clerk. Amazingly, the immediate response was a job offer at Waikune Prison in National Park in the North Island. A house went with the job. I didn't question why a clerk with unexceptional scholastic achievements should be so much in demand for work in a prison camp in the middle of nowhere. I was to find out later that this was not so much because the Department of Justice was impressed with my skills. They could not find anyone in New Zealand willing to go to such a location. I went into the public library in Oxford to see what I could find out about National Park. It seemed to be in the mountainous area in the centre of the North Island near somewhere called the Desert Road. There was a railway station at National Park, but the nearest settlement was a place called Erua and the nearest town was Taumarunui, about twenty-five miles away. Auckland was about two hundred miles north and Wellington, the capital, was about two hundred miles south.

If the New Zealand Government was going to pay my fare, the next step was outside the hands of the Department of Justice. I had to go to New Zealand House for an interview with someone from the Immigration Service. The official record of this interview ends with a summary dated 6 September 1965:

Applicant is a neatly dressed, sincere young man. He has a cheerful friendly personality and a confident polished manner. He is keen on a career in this type of work. He impresses as being level headed, mature, honest and of high integrity.

Mrs Farrell has recently given birth to a child and was unable to attend the interview. We shall arrange to see her in the near future.

We duly returned a few days later so they could check Brenda and Nick, although we were not quite sure what response the Immigration Service expected from a ten day old child. What is not recorded in the two-page record of my interview is the reaction from the interviewing officer when I showed him my offer of a job at Waikune Prison in National Park.

"Jesus Christ," he said, laughing. "National Park? That is the arsehole of New Zealand. If you last two years there, you can live anywhere."

Things were beginning to move at speed. We were accepted by the New Zealand Government as assisted immigrants, provided I took the job at Waikune Prison. The Department of Justice was also offering a house at Waikune and wanted me to fly out before Christmas, ahead of Brenda and the baby. Fly out! I had never been on a plane, and most immigrants who travelled to New Zealand then went by the long sea route. A few days later a job offer from the Commonwealth Relations Office arrived.

I was elated with these demands for my services, but we did not have to accept either of them – we could just stay put. We did not play it safe; we did not make a list of pros and cons. I am always thankful to Brenda for gently but firmly edging us into the decision just to go with what we felt was right. She would be left on her own to sell the house and learn about the mysteries of motherhood while I flew out to the other side of the world.

My grandmother had thirteen children but the family I was to leave behind in England had been fragmented and shrunk considerably. Only Agnes, Mum's eldest sister, had remained in the East End although even she had moved away from Barrington Road after Uncle George died. When we went to see her to say goodbye, she was confused about what was happening. The landscape around her was changing in every respect. Bleak high-rise apartment blocks were replacing the bomb-damaged housing and post-war prefab buildings in her part of the East End. New immigrants were flooding in.

"We only used to see darkies when Sam from Barrington Road came first-footing at New Year. Now, they're everywhere." It was just an observation, not a judgement of any sort. She didn't have any particular concerns. She was just puzzled and a bit lonely.

Some goodbyes were easy. Others were not. It was as if some people understood the enormity of the step we were taking. Others had little interest in what was going on beyond the shores of Mother England, and leaving was somehow unpatriotic. We promised to send forwarding addresses, and they promised to keep in touch. I wrote to Shaw to tell him we were leaving for New Zealand, but he did not reply.

It was dark at 4.00pm when I left for Heathrow. Sleet settled as ice in the corners of the bus windows as I peered out for my last look at England. It would be a few months before I would see Brenda and the baby again. Leaving them even for such a short time had left me empty and apprehensive. It had been a wise decision to forego airport farewells as it gave me some time to compose myself for what was ahead. The overheated terminal was bright with the lights of Christmas. A choir of young children in school uniform was assembled around a Christmas tree, singing carols. Some families had stopped to join in. It was as if I was a visitor from another world, just watching but not feeling a part of anything that was going on around me. I had never been to an air terminal before. This was quite a different place from the Maidstone bus station. Scanning the mysterious places on the departure board, I found the BOAC flight BA722 to Auckland. It was to be a thirty-six hour journey with stops at Rome, Bombay and Darwin. It was too late for second thoughts.

It was hot and sticky when I arrived at Auckland Airport. Christmas belonged in the cold and dark. Not in that place, where sharp summer light presided over barbecues and cicadas rather than snowmen and chestnuts. Doris Day and Dean Martin Christmas songs were being played through the public address system.

"G'day. Mr Farrell, is it? Got your passport?" The voice was friendly enough, if a little brisk.

It wasn't the welcome I expected, but the New Zealand Immigration Service had to protect the government's investment. I handed over my mint condition United Kingdom passport with its one lonely entry, which had been stamped *Permitted to enter: 20 December 1965* when I passed through New Zealand Customs.

The young man from immigration looked over the document and casually slipped it inside his briefcase. He had a ruddy outdoors face, cropped blond hair and blank, disinterested eyes. With his thick thighs crowded into grey shorts and long woollen socks, there was an air of a truculent sixth former about him.

"Ta. You'll get this back after two years. Here's your receipt, your bus chit to the railway station and your ticket for the train to National Park. That's the nearest station for Waikune Prison. I hate these weekend pick-ups," he said, using immigration jargon that was quite beyond me. "A joker doesn't get a weekend to himself. Still, at least you speak English." He smiled happily at his own joke.

At that point, I had not uttered a word. I was about to become very good at keeping my own counsel.

"You can catch the bus out the front. Takes about an hour. Then it's a short walk to the railway station. Train doesn't leave until seven so you've got plenty of time." His face softened. "Best of luck. You'll need it where you're going."

"So I've been told," I replied lightly, as I gathered my bags and moved off to find the bus. The air outside the terminal was clear and the sun hot against my face, pale from the northern winter.

Auckland Railway Station was cavernous and much quieter than I expected. The departure of the train to Wellington seemed to be the highlight of the day as passengers began to gather around the far platform. Their excited chatter echoed across empty platforms. I walked past the red weather-beaten railway carriages looking for my seat. The train was crowded. There was a smell of fish and chips and beer as families settled in for the long overnight journey to Wellington. My last meal had been served up by BOAC somewhere over Darwin. There didn't seem to be a dining car. Not that I had any cash; I only had a few UK pounds left from the money we had allocated from our savings.

Soon, most of the passengers were asleep. The setting sun played through the windows as we rattled towards Hamilton. Somewhere a guitar was being gently strummed. The Christmas carol was familiar, but incongruous to me in those surroundings.

"Next stop National Park," the guard announced as he moved through the darkened carriage, torch in hand. Five hours after we had left Auckland, the train heaved and shook as we pulled out of Taumarunui. Anxious that I would miss the stop, I lifted my cases down, stumbled over the snoring, farting bodies next to mine and struggled towards the exit door where I stood, waiting. It took the train a further hour to labour up the Raurimu spiral towards the central plateau of mountains. I wiped the steamy window, forehead against the cold glass, peering into the night. Through the darkness there were glimpses of dark green foliage, glistening wet. Lowering the window, I caught what would become the familiar sweet dank smell of the New Zealand bush. I thought of Brenda and the baby in London. I was glad they weren't with me.

Steam and smoke poured from the black engine as it halted at National Park Station. I jumped down onto a dark empty platform, shining and slippery with the early morning dew. I had been rehearsing this moment in my head ever since I left Heathrow.

The train clattered off into the darkness. A railway-crossing bell rang out in the distance, and then there was a deep empty silence. The station buildings were in darkness, save for a flickering light bulb illuminating what looked like a ticket office. The office was empty. I pushed open the exit door and looked around outside, confident there would be some transport for me. The landscape was overwhelming. Etched black against the sky was the unmistakable shape of a volcano. I was a Lilliputian confronted by Gulliver's world. There wasn't a soul there, not even a ticket collector. I shivered against the cold mountain air and drew my new Marks and Spencer duffel coat around me. My sense of arrival and alienation were complete.

There was a black wind-up phone in the ticket office. The operator chattered away as she connected me to the prison number. I got the impression she had not had a call to deal with all night. There was an unfamiliar lilt to her voice. Could it be Māori? She didn't charge me for the call.

"Waikune Prison." The owner of the voice was obviously none too pleased at being awakened at that time in the morning.

"It's Peter Farrell." I thought that a laconic and easy-going image should find acceptance.

"Who?"

"Peter Farrell."

"There's no Peter Farrell here, mate."

"No. Sorry. *I'm* Peter Farrell. I'm starting work there tomorrow," I said. I had done my research and knew the first rule for being accepted – always avoid any reference to England and never, ever, make unfavourable comparisons.

"You the new Pom?"

"Yes. I've just come off the Auckland train. There doesn't seem to be any transport up here. The station's all closed up."

"Not surprised. Old Ron usually gets pissed on Fridays." Ron must be the stationmaster, I thought. "It's not bloody Piccadilly Circus, mate. I suppose you're expecting a taxi." The edge had returned to his voice.

"Nah, don't worry about it. I'll just bunk down here till morning," I said, eyeing the old wooden station bench doubtfully.

"No need to do that. They left the camp van up there somewhere for you. The keys will be in it. Just go up to the main road and turn right. It'll take you about half an hour." He seemed to have relaxed a bit.

"I don't have a New Zealand licence." I didn't like to admit that I had no driving licence of any sort, having failed my test three times on the twisting country roads around Grendon Underwood.

He reverted to his earlier dismissive tone. "Christ. I sometimes wonder how you bastards ever won the war. Just find the bloody van and drive it. We'll sort out the paperwork later."

The Bedford van was some distance from the station. *New Zealand Government* was painted in white on the grey bodywork, and the door was pitted with rust. I loaded on my bags and nervously climbed into the cab. I found the ignition and the van coughed into life. Co-ordinating the clutch and gears had always been my downfall, and I stalled the motor twice before pulling away in a spray of gravel. By the time I got to the main road I discovered which of the mysterious switches turned the lights on. Then, unencumbered by any other traffic, I found my confidence growing.

The headlights picked out a narrow unsurfaced road. The occasional wisp of foliage reached out of the bush and trailed against the windscreen. By the time I swung into the prison camp, I felt I could easily be mistaken for an experienced driver. Waikune was a low security prison; but for the floodlit compound, the prison buildings had the appearance of a large, unkempt motel rather than a prison. Prisoners were evidently locked down and checked at night, but there were no walls or fences. The authorities obviously felt the inhospitable mountain bush surrounding the prison for miles around was containment enough.

I saw smoke spiralling up from the wooden houses dotted around the perimeter of the compound. A few grey trucks were parked carelessly there. I followed the lights to what looked like a reception area and jumped down from the van. There was a smell of bacon in the air. This was to be home.

A blue-uniformed figure emerged from the reception area. "Welcome. I'm Colin." He smiled and shook my hand. This was the owner of the clipped, irritable voice on the phone. He was far less intimidating in person.

"I'll show you to the single jokers' quarters. That's where we eat. Breakfast is in half an hour." He took one of my bags and ambled off with me in tow.

With no wife in evidence, I was to be treated as a single joker. This meant I had my own room in the single men's compound, but that was to be the limit of my privacy. The single men's quarters looked like a modern extension of the prison itself. Each tiny room had an identical layout with an iron bedstead, a sink and a wooden desk. There was no chair. One wall of the room I was shown into was plastered with curling, sun-faded posters of Dusty Springfield. I was a long way from the London Palladium and beehive hairdos. I unpacked my suitcase. It didn't take long. It was time to go in for breakfast.

"I'm Henry." The inmate kitchenhand was immaculately turned out in carefully pressed whites. "I do the breakfast cooking for the jokers coming off the night shift. What do you want? We got mince, lamb chops, eggs, anything really. He fussed over the stainless steel trays, waiting for my answer. "You must be absolutely stuffed after all that travel." He seemed concerned. I was hardly Captain Cook, but it was good to have someone acknowledge the extent of my journey.

Henry was the only inmate allowed in the single officers' quarters. I was 'the new Pom'. We were both outsiders. I was soon to learn a lot from him about how to fit in with my new colleagues.

15

PRISON LIFE

There were four other men spread around a large formica table that could probably have taken about sixteen or so if needed. They all talked around, through and above me, as if I wasn't there. Their conversation was full of prison in-jokes and jargon, and there were a lot of provocative references to England, thrown out like some sort of lure. I had expected some of this, but there was an underlying menace that was unnerving. I smiled along with them but managed to avoid rising to the bait.

There was a clattering from the kitchen, interspersed with much cursing. A large young man pushed Henry to one side and emerged with two plates in each hand. He smashed them down at the place beside me. Grey porridge slopped around one plate. The other plate contained two fat-rimmed mutton chops sitting on top of thick fried bread. He swung his legs over the wooden bench and placed himself down between me and the others, elbows nudging into my ribs as he shovelled porridge and chops indiscriminately into his mouth. When he finished, he belched comfortably and turned to me as if noticing my presence for the first time. The smell of mutton fat was heavy on his breath.

"I'm Baz. Waddya think of the tucker?"

I shrugged carefully. "It's okay."

"Ooooh, it's okay is it?" Baz brayed in what he saw as high camp English. He flapped a loose right wrist to the others in case anyone round the table was in doubt about the insult that had been delivered. "Hear that, Henry?" He called into the kitchen. "This new joker must be one of yours. Bet you can't wait to get your hands on him!"

He reached into his mouth and pulled out a full set of false teeth and placed them in front of me. Mutton gristle and small globs of chewed fried bread were still attached to the teeth. Warm saliva seeped onto the table. If I had said anything at all or attempted to return his gaze, the baiting would have continued. Baz eventually heaved himself upwards, slotted his teeth back into his mouth. "Bloody Poms. You bastards are all the same," he said jovially, as if it'd all been a joke. He pushed me in the back and left. The others soon followed without saying anything further to me.

Henry had watched this exchange. "Don't worry about that lot. They are always a bit shitty when they come off the night shift. The boss said no need to start today, you probably want to get some sleep yourself after that trip." I thought it was a bit odd that the superintendent had passed this message through Henry, but I had a lot to learn about how things worked here and whom you could trust.

That night, secure in my own room, I gave way to a bout of homesickness. I started a letter to Brenda. The hurt and misery poured out onto the page. I didn't know how to tell her that we had made a dreadful mistake. The big adventure was turning into a nightmare. There was a hammering on the door. I screwed the letter up and composed myself before slipping back the bolt. The man standing there was huge. His face was ravaged and puffy, with the highlight being a large red bulbous nose set between a pair of ears slapped like underdone steaks on either side of his head. His hair was very much short back and sides. He looked like one of Nick's Mr Wobbly cuddle toys. Indeed, for all his size, the man before me did have some of Mr Wobbly's quizzical, self-satisfied features.

"Yeah. Gidday. I'm Frank," he said. His handshake was crushing, but he did not meet my eyes.

He removed his boots and moved into the room on thick stockinged feet, the curiously polite ritual employed by all single jokers on entering the room of another. There was nowhere for him to sit apart from the bed and that was somehow too intimate. He perched on the windowsill and seemed to fill the room. He rolled a smoke, concentrating hard, the tiny white paper lost in large hairy fingers.

"A few of us jokers go up to the club after work. Want me to pick you up tomorrow?" I was soon to learn that National Park had a pub, an RSA and a Cosmopolitan Club. The 'Cozzie Club' was clearly where everyone from the prison went.

The club was a corrugated iron shed with a large black pot-bellied stove set in the middle of the floor. The air was thick with its smoke and the acrid, invasive smell of tobacco. I looked around quickly to locate the bar to make sure I got there ahead of Frank. I needed to ensure that I got my round in first.

Some others joined us. Much to my relief, there was no sign of Baz or any of the night shift group from breakfast. Soon more beer jugs appeared on the table. I noticed the way they held their six-ounce glasses, thumb horizontal and fingers somehow splayed downwards and away. It seemed to facilitate the maximum dispatch of beer down the throat with the most economical jerk of the arm. The minutiae of prison life were the main topics of conversation. Women were also the subject of much discussion and speculation, although there was not a woman to be seen anywhere. I was able to relax into a companionable, alcohol-induced anonymity, although I did wonder how we were going to drink the three or four jugs of beer in the allotted time before Dave, the cop, arrived to close the place down at 6.30pm. All bars were required to close at 6.00pm in those days, but Dave knew his patch well enough to allow a little flexibility. Conversation slowed down for the last half hour as full attention turned to dispatching the jugs of beer on the table. I began to feel sick and dizzy and was very relieved when Dave turned up in his blue uniform. He was used to the ironic cheering that greeted his appearance at closing time, but everyone trooped out without complaint.

We had a couple of stops on the way home to piss at the side of the road. An obvious post Cozzie Club ritual. There were grunts and crude comments as we steamed up the cold night air. Nobody spoke directly to me, which was just as well, as I doubted that I was sober enough to form any coherent words. Thanks to Frank, I felt that my temporary single joker status had received some sort of endorsement, although there was still Baz and his smorgasbord of prejudices to be managed somehow.

If that was what I had to do every night till Brenda arrived, so be it. I giggled drunkenly at the thought of myself pissing with my mates in the shadow of a volcano just one week after those formal farewells in England. I had lived in and around institutions all of my life. This one had its idiosyncrasies, but I thought I would be able to survive, and that was an important first step.

I reported for work the next day. The Superintendent was an ebullient, slightly built man who seemed to enjoy his control over the small, incestuous prison community.

"John Brown is starting as the Senior Clerk after Christmas, so you'll be on your own till then, although we do have a temp working in there, someone else out from UK. Sid, I think his name is." He spoke briskly. I detected a southern English accent but could not place it closer than that. He had deceptively open, blue eyes. "I don't know why head office got you out here so soon. The place runs on auto pilot over the Christmas period."

"Everything okay in the quarters?" He looked down at some papers on his desk without waiting for a reply. "You've got a family coming out in a couple of months. Is that right?"

"The quarters are fine, but I would be quite happy to move into the house." Housing was included in the whole deal, as it was for all staff employed in such a remote location. "I'd like to get things ready for when they come out. Who do I need to talk to about that?"

"I approve all the staff housing allocations. There's nothing available at the moment, but there's no hurry," he said dismissively. There was an uncomfortable silence. "Quite frankly Peter, you'll need to be careful here if you start making demands about housing. It's a very sensitive issue and could put you offside with a few people." My mistrust of anyone who prefaces what they are about to say with 'quite frankly' or 'frankly' dates from that moment. I heard the warning, but for me housing was too important an issue to leave completely to this man's dispensation of grace and favour.

There was a relaxed air around the prison as preparations were under way for Christmas. There was nothing to do in the office, so I went up to the main compound to try and make myself useful. There were a few in the guardroom who nodded to me in recognition, having seen me at the Cozzie Club the night before.

"Anyone got anything Peter here can do? There's fuck all for him in the office at the moment." The officer in charge punctuated every sentence at least once with the word 'fuck' or 'fucking'. The word itself wasn't so shocking to me, but I soon found myself enthralled to see exactly when and how many times he would manage to insert the word into any given sentence.

"I'm getting some tucker together for Christmas lunch he can help me with." Gordon was a quietly spoken man in white denims. "You okay working with boobheads?" There was a whole lexicon of prison slang to learn, on both sides of the fence. 'Boob' was the prison, therefore 'boobheads' were prison inmates. "Yes, that's fine." I hadn't had any briefing on security or anything so I just followed Gordon, assuming he would tell me anything I needed to know. He took me over the tar sealed compound to the kitchen store. The sun beat down on our backs. Inside, the store was dark and cool. Two inmates were in there. They both wore khaki shirts, cutaway shorts and what looked like sandals. (I later found these were called 'jandals'.) They were bent over a short trestle table with a plastic cloth stretched across it. They seemed to be arranging an array of small brown paper bags alongside some biscuit tins which contained rich-smelling Christmas cake.

"This is Peter Farrell, the new joker in the office." They straightened up, smiling. "This is Sam Manu." He pointed to the thicker set of the two. Sam was Māori. He had sunglasses tucked up into his thick black hair. "And this is Mitch Mitchell." Mitch was a slightly built older man. He didn't seem as interested in his appearance as Sam. His shorts were longer and flapped against his skinny pale legs. Both men nodded companionably enough at me.

"They'll show you what to do," Gordon said and left the store. I looked after him wondering whether I had been set up. I knew the place was minimum security, but this was not quite what I had been used to. There was no reaction from my two new workmates, so I awaited their instructions. It was a simple enough job, cutting up the large slabs of cake and putting the smaller cuts, into each paper bag. We then had to tag each bag from the handwritten list that contained the names of all the inmates who would be at the Christmas dinner the next day. Many of the names were Māori. Sam laughed good-naturedly as I struggled to pronounce names like 'Watene', 'Maniapoto' and 'Te Teko'.

It was getting cold inside the store so we moved outside for what they called 'smoko'. We sat on a wooden bench in the sun while Sam rolled a cigarette. His large brown tattooed fingers caressed the light paper before running a surprisingly delicate pink tongue along the seam to seal in the tobacco. His sunglasses remained nestled in his hair although the afternoon sun was shining directly down on us.

"This place a bit different than what you're used to, eh boss?" It was a rhetorical question. I just smiled and nodded. "When your family coming out? They tell me you are a family man? How many kids you got?"

Word had obviously got out. "Couple of months before they get here," I replied. "We've just had a baby. Our first."

"I got an idea for when mum and the kid get out here, boss. I could be your houseboy." He smiled as he saw me trying to work out what a houseboy could possibly be.

"It's all above board. All the screws do it. Might as well be part of it, eh?" His eyes narrowed slyly. "It's easy. I do a bit of work for you and mum, after work in here finishes. I could stack some wood, dig the garden, that sort of thing. Just costs you a packet of twenty and everybody's happy. I get some tailor-mades to trade off for figs with the other boobheads, and you and mum get some work done around the place."

He squinted at the finished product before popping it in the battered tin with the rest of his collection. From what he had told me back in the store, he wouldn't be out until 1969, two years away. He was not in any hurry.

I now knew what a 'houseboy' was. Using what universal prison slang I had already picked up at Grendon and Holloway, I also knew that 'screws' were prison officers and 'tailor-mades' were packet cigarettes. I was later to work out that 'figs' were the tobacco scrapings that were packed into small plastic bags and sold in the prison canteen. 'Mum' was the name given to the woman who shared your bed every night, rather than the woman who gave you life.

'Boss' was used by the inmates to address anyone in any sort of authority who might need a bit of flattery. The term didn't sit very comfortably with my expectations of an egalitarian society, but this was prison and sticking your head up above the parapet would not be a wise move.

Sam was waiting for my answer. "I'll have to see how it all works Sam then I'll get back to you."

Sam shrugged. "Okay boss," he said.

As it turned out, Sam's description of the role of a houseboy was correct. The Superintendent had up to five houseboys assigned to his large white wooden house. I never did see inside his house, but apparently the houseboys did all the jobs that Sam described and would also clean the house and wait at the table. Many of the staff houses had inmates working in them in some part-time capacity or other. Sam was right, everybody seemed to win in the deal as long as nobody was particularly concerned about exploitation or the security issues involved. I was glad I could postpone making a decision on our involvement until Brenda got there.

I didn't like the prospect of spending Christmas in the single officers' quarters and there was going to be no work for me in the office. Sid, the English boy working as a temp in the office, was planning to hitchhike to Napier on the East Coast for a couple of days to break the monotony. He asked me to join him. So, on Christmas Day, we signed out at the guardhouse and got a lift in a prison truck going to one of the other prisons over at Tūrangi on the other side of the mountains. From there it only took four or five hours to get to Napier. We found somewhere to stay for two nights. On Boxing Day, we went to the North Island Roller Skating Championships at the rink on Marine Parade. It rained in the afternoon so we went to see the latest Beatles movie. By then we had just about exhausted the attractions of Napier for two young men with no money, no car and no local knowledge, so we hitchhiked back to the prison the next day.

Henry was watching out for us when we arrived at the single officers' mess. "You're in the shit," he said, looking at me sympathetically. "The boss came here looking for you yesterday. I think he's pissed off that you didn't tell him you weren't going to be here over Christmas."

"We told them in the guardroom we were going and when we would be back. What more does he want?" In my anxiety I forgot who Henry was and not to get him involved in this.

"Dunno, but you had better be ready for a bollocking tomorrow. He was ropeable about you only being here five minutes and then buggering off out." I was indignant at the injustice of it all but backed off. It would only make matters worse if I said anything else to Henry, who seemed sympathetic but was also enjoying his role as the bearer of bad news.

I went to see the Superintendent first thing in the morning.

"Hello, Peter. Had a good Christmas?" He was all reason.

"Yes thanks. Henry in the quarters tells me that you were looking for me." I kept my voice level.

"I was over there looking for you on Boxing Day. Just wanted to see how you were getting on. How was Napier?"

The expected bollocking did not come. I did not believe he had been checking up on my welfare. However, the Superintendent had absolute power over all staff and inmates, and if he chose to operate in a certain way, there was not much I could do about it.

"Napier was good," I said, and left it at that.

The two months before Brenda and the baby arrived allowed me to establish myself in the job and gain some acceptance around the place. John, the new Senior Clerk, arrived after Christmas. He was Māori and had moved up from Wellington to be nearer his people at Tokaanu, near Tūrangi. John had never worked in a prison environment before but I learned a lot more from him and his wife Kath than he did from me. There was an apparent casualness about his approach that hid a real thoroughness towards his work. Some of John's responses were not always what I would expect, which I found confusing. I was later to spend more time with him out of work and came to realise how he and Kath managed themselves between two cultures.

I lived the life of a single joker to the full during those two months. The visits to the Cozzie Club continued. Sometimes I would get an invitation from one of the married jokers to go home for tea. I learned not to accept these alcohol-fuelled invitations at short notice at the Cozzie Club, as this could mean my arriving unannounced and not particularly welcome by the woman of the house. There was one occasion when I stood swaying drunkenly in the washhouse while my host entered into a furious negotiation with his wife about my presence. Voices were raised in stage whispers.

Her: "You should have bloody told me you were bringing him home."

Him: "Poor bugger is separated from his family. Just give him a feed. He won't stay long."

I just wanted to get out of there, but that would have made things worse.

Having watched a couple of games involving the prison rugby team, I decided to give that a miss. My short stint at what they called rugby at Eltham College bore no relationship to the ferocity of the New Zealand version that played out in front of me.

I did accept an invitation to go night spotlighting, although I was not quite sure what that meant. Taz was in charge of forestry operations for the three prisons that occupied the volcanic plateau. He was a huge man. When he climbed into the Land Rover, the vehicle tipped significantly to the driver's side. Our companion in the passenger seat was a sad-faced man called Jock. There was no burr of Scotland in his accent, but there was a whiff of stale Scotch on his breath. I climbed into the platform at the back which started a cacophony of barking from the two fearsome-looking dogs that were chained up there. I shrank into the corner behind the driver's seat, making sure I was beyond striking distance from those yellow jaws.

"We just drive up Old Baldy," Jock said, referring to the small mountain that rose up behind the prison. "By the time we get in there it should be quite dark. We'll turn on the spotlights and see what we can see. If we get a pig lined up we'll release the dogs on him."

I nodded, not quite sure about the implications for me in what I was hearing.

"Your rifle is under the muslin cloth down by your feet somewhere. The catch'll be on." I pulled at the cloth and saw the rifle lying there. I had seen plenty of guns waved around by Richard Widmark and Henry Fonda in the westerns I used to see at the Granada in Maidstone, but I couldn't remember actually seeing a real rifle. I certainly hadn't touched one before. I lifted it gingerly and put it across my knees. It was surprisingly light and smelt of grease.

"There should be a couple of pig sticks there somewhere," Jock said.

I scrabbled around and found two short steel rods. Each had what looked like a crudely fashioned wooden handle at one end. The other end had been filed down to a wicked sharp point. "Keep those handy as we might need them. If it all goes to plan, the dogs will hold the pig down by the ears and we'll push the stick into the bugger's heart. If that doesn't work, we'll shoot him." I felt my own heart lurch with dread at what I'd got myself into.

We started on the bumpy track into the bush. I was worried the rifle would slip off my knees, so I moved it back onto the floor with the barrel facing away from me. Taz and Jock carried out a running commentary for my benefit, but I found it difficult to hear what they were saying over the roar of the engine. I looked across at the dogs. Quieter now, they were eyeing me keenly, their squat grey bodies straining at their chains, dribble splashing from their jowls. It was as if they sensed that this Pom knew absolutely nothing about hunting.

God answered my silent prayer that night. We drove through the bush for three hours without seeing anything. Much to my relief, they decided to return home. Once Brenda got there and I could become a responsible married joker, I would be able to turn down all such invitations.

I wrote encouraging and optimistic letters back home to Brenda, but as the time ran down to her arrival, I began to wonder whether we had done the right thing. The work was not particularly interesting. The weather was variable, blinding sun and pouring rain, often on the same day. Beautiful though it was, National Park was beginning to live up to the billing given it by the immigration officer in London. Most of all, I was still trying to get a decision from the superintendent about the accommodation that had been promised as part of the agreement. The more I pressed, the more evasive he became. Two weeks before Brenda and the baby were due to get on the plane for New Zealand, I was shown an old possum trapper's cottage set deep in the bush near Erua, about four kilometres south of the prison. The ground outside had flooded from a recent downpour and access was restricted to some old wooden boards laid down to the front door. Nobody had lived in it for a while and once I got inside there were signs of rats and the smell of something very rotten. I was told it wouldn't take much to get power in there from the main road.

"I'm sorry, Tom, I didn't sign up to that." I was in the Superintendent's office once more. "We couldn't possibly put a young child in a place like that. And it wouldn't be fair to my wife to manage in such a remote situation with no guaranteed power or telephone."

"I told you we could easily get power and a phone in there, Peter." I knew I was going to get a repeat of the lecture about being grateful I'd got any accommodation laid on at all and that if I got too demanding I could put myself offside within the community. The lecture duly arrived, but by this time, I was more established and less willing to be compliant. Also, I was desperate.

"I'm happy to put this in the hands of the head office people in Wellington, as they signed off this letter with all the conditions about housing." I was shaking as I put the letter in front of him. I knew he would have had a copy anyway. This was the biggest risk I had ever taken in my fairly risk-free life to date. "Otherwise I will just have to ring UK and tell my wife to hold off coming until this can be sorted." I had worked out that if I ratcheted this up to a higher authority, it might take it out of his control. Wellington was a long way from National Park, but upsetting head office could sometimes have unfortunate repercussions for a superintendent.

His face coloured, and I thought he was going to explode. Instead, he widened his eyes, smiled gently and said, "Quite frankly, Peter, you are being totally unreasonable after everything that has been done for you. I will have another look and see what I can do, but you need to know that I will not be held to ransom over this." I knew then that even if this ever got resolved, he would not forget this incident.

Later the next day, I heard from John that some temporary accommodation had been secured for us at National Park, near the police house. I knew the cottage. It had been used by a forester until quite recently. It had mains power, a septic tank and roof rainwater as well as a coal range, so it would do for us for a while. I also knew that Dave, the cop, and Ruth, his wife, would be our next door neighbours, so I agreed to the arrangement. The subject of housing was never again raised by the Superintendent.

With housing at last sorted, I could prepare for the arrival of Brenda and Nick. In my last few letters home, I had deliberately tried to dampen down Brenda's expectations. She was pale and tired when she came off the plane at Auckland Airport. We stayed overnight in Auckland before embarking on the long train trip to National Park. At least I was able to ensure that our arrival there was a bit more welcoming than mine had been three months previously. Dave and Ruth had prepared supper for us, and then we went to the cottage that was to be our home for six months until more permanent accommodation was available. I was a bit apprehensive about how Brenda would react to the tiny cottage. I should not have worried. I had married someone whose stoicism and powers of adaptation exceeded my own. Nick, then only six months old, was less comfortable in his new surroundings on the other side of the world. He took months to adjust to the different feeding times that applied in the southern hemisphere.

In New Zealand, everyone spoke English, cars drove on the left-hand side of the road and laws were similar to what we were used to. Yet, in subtle ways, New Zealand was a foreign country full of potential pitfalls to us. Brenda and I grew strong by drawing upon one another's resources. We could whinge and complain to one another about some minor setback but tried to keep clear of the 'moaning Pom' tag that was so easily earned and so difficult to shed. Gradually we built up a small circle of friends, mostly off the prison site, in National Park or Taumarunui, who we could trust with our frustrations.

By the time we had permanent accommodation on the prison staff housing estate, I had the job of telling Sam that we would not take him up on his offer to be our houseboy. He was on the forestry truck that was delivering wood to the staff houses. We were standing by a pile of rough-cut timber, which had been dropped in the back garden. "Suit yourself, boss," he had shrugged. "But you'll need to make sure you get your wood stacked up before the winter." It was still late summer, and I foolishly did not listen to his warning or realise the implications of the snowline moving down Mt Ruapehu as the season changed to autumn. The winters in National Park were brutal. Each evening I looked gloomily at the pile of snow in the garden. It was a monument to my incompetence and my penance was simple. Each morning I would scrape the snow from the pile, pull out a barrow load of wood and take it into the house to dry in the electric stove so it was ready to burn on the open fire in the evening. During that first winter I returned home from work to an overwhelming smell of drying wood. I learned my lesson. The next year I was proudly showing everyone my beautifully stacked woodshed. In much the same way, Brenda took great pleasure in showing off her beautifully stacked bottled apricots. Our assimilation was almost complete.

We were able to juggle our parenting duties to enable Brenda to get herself a part-time job at the telephone switchboard in National Park. This gave her a crash course in the pronunciation of Māori place names. My own job was going well, and I found myself sent over to other prisons in the North Island to relieve from time to time.

One Monday morning Scouse started work as a cleaner in the office at Waikune. With his close-cropped hair, steely grey eyes and menacing self-contained demeanour, he was regarded as a bit of a hard man.

If he been satisfied just to desert ship, he would have spent a few weeks in Mount Crawford Prison in Wellington and then been popped on a ship home to Liverpool. Unfortunately, nobody had told him about six o'clock closing. So when the cops came to close down the Lambton Quay bar at the allotted time, Scouse did not take kindly to the interruption. "I just nutted a few of them," he once told me. Scouse was one of a number of long-termers seeing out their last few months in the more relaxed environment of a prison camp.

"You hear the results yesterday?" His nasal accent was slick and oily. The question was like a freemasonic handshake. The UK football results were read out after the news on the National Programme on Sunday mornings at 9am. Listening to the prim announcer trying to get his tongue around mystifying names like Accrington Stanley, Stenhousemuir and Leyton Orient was a highlight of my week in those first few years. It was a tenuous link with home and a reminder of how far away I was from familiar places.

"Yeah, I heard them, West Ham lost at home again." I knew a fellow sufferer when I saw one. Scouse nodded in sympathy.

"How did Tranmere get on?" he asked tentatively. "They were away at Queens Park Rangers." The hard grey eyes softened, he knew the news would be bad. He was like a pit bull terrier, awaiting inevitable punishment.

"Lost 4-0." It was my turn to commiserate. Each Monday from then until he was released, we enjoyed a brief mutual support session. Both of us had our own reasons for hanging on to a past life.

In rural communities like Waikune, 'going to town' was quite an event. I took the prison van in to Taumarunui every Friday. The official reason was to get supplies, but many of the women also travelled into town to do shopping and to attend personal appointments. It was a pleasant drive when the weather was fine, and Taumarunui had all the basics of a small town. I did most of the prison shopping in the local grocery store at the far end of town and got to know the proprietor well. One day when I was at the checkout, he waved me over.

"You're a Pom aren't you?" I nodded, flattered that he had to ask. "You people like these things don't you? They're really difficult to get." He pulled his hand from under the counter, looked cautiously over his shoulder and opened his big fist. There, nestling in his hand, was a small red package of Oxo cubes.

"Wow, it's a while since I've seen one of those," I said, wondering what was coming next. It's true that some immigrants had a craving for Oxo cubes. Our particular craving was for sausages or McVitie's chocolate wheaten biscuits, but I thought it best not to tell him that.

"Well," he said, smiling. "Seeing you are bringing so much business in here, I thought I would shout you one." He opened the red package and extracted one tiny silver-wrapped cube and pushed it towards me.

I wondered about telling him it was more than my job was worth to accept inducements, but I decided against it. "Thanks so much for thinking of us. You've made our Sunday lunch." He beamed with pleasure.

The trip to town the next week was also memorable, although for a different reason. Bluey Weatherson was an inmate. He was also a painter and a thief. He had been doing some painting work around the office but hadn't been able to finish it because his release date came up. He had left on the previous Wednesday. On Friday I was in town as usual and called in to the Bank of New South Wales in Miriama Street. Inside there were painters' dropcloths all over the place and a stepladder propped against the wall. A familiar figure was bent over a large can of paint. "Bluey?" I said. The figure straightened up.

"How you going boss? You got that painting done yet?" There was a bit of a challenge in his smile. I knew he was not on parole, and he had done his time. If the bank had hired him, they presumably had done some checking. I decided to let it rest.

"You take care, Bluey," I said, looking meaningfully at him. I was relieved that there was no news about bank robberies in Taumarunui in the weeks that followed. We had to wait nine months to get the painting completed. Bluey was eventually caught doing a burglary in Hamilton and returned to finish the job.

The Waikune environment was generally very relaxed. Inmates at the end of long sentences or those serving reasonably short periods of imprisonment were not going to risk 'going back up the line' for some misdemeanour or other. There was the occasional escape, but generally the inhospitable mountain bush proved containment enough unless someone found a way to jump onto a train as it slowed down going up the gradient to National Park. Sometimes the alarm siren would scream at night for a major disturbance, usually involving too much consumption of home brew.

One of the few times there was a police cordon on the road to Taumarunui was the night we thought our second child was being born. We were a bit concerned when we got waved down in case they wanted to search the car.

"There's been an escape," said the voice behind the torchlight shining into the car. He must have been one of the cops from town. I didn't know him but I had heard the sirens at the prison earlier in the evening. We were too preoccupied to worry about that. The cop waved us through hurriedly when he heard where we were going and why.

"Don't stop for anybody," he said. Fat chance.

We later found out the inmate had panicked once he left the prison and hid in the bush at the side of the road before giving himself up the next morning. The cops didn't believe he had been in the bush all night. They thought he had gone into the pub at National Park although they couldn't smell anything on his breath. He only convinced them he was telling the truth when he gave them a detailed account of watching them race frogs in the middle of State Highway one.

That trip to Taumarunui proved to be a false alarm and we had to repeat the journey a week later. Our daughter Kay was eventually born in the hospital on 20 October 1967, a real New Zealander. We had become a family with a son and a daughter. All around us there were families who knew what they were doing. Dave and Ruth had a boy and two girls and seemed hugely competent. My boss John and his wife Kath, who were living up the road from us, also had a boy and a girl. There were occasions when their children's nana swooped in and took the mokopuna away for months on end. This seemed shocking to us at the time, but on reflection, we would have been very pleased to have had some release from twenty-four hour parenting. Forty-five kilometres away, in Taumarunui, our friends Alan and Marjorie, immigrants like us, knew exactly what they were doing and they had four children. In the absence of a nana, *Dr Spock's Baby and Child Care* became our de facto adviser and guide on all aspects of parenting. As a back-up to Dr Spock, there was always the instinct to protect and nurture these dependent beings we loved so much.

There was a changing of the guard at Waikune Prison. The appointment of a new Superintendent gave me an opportunity to start with a clean sheet. The new man's arrival coincided with what was then the first significant volcanic activity on Mt Ruapehu for many years. Plumes of smoke poured from the mountain. There were reports of the crater lake rising and warnings of a possible onrush of molten lava. The volunteer fire brigades in National Park and Taumarunui were put on alert. How much help they would be with the prospect of molten lava tumbling down the side of the mountain, nobody quite knew. Brenda and I had by then obtained our drivers' licences, so we left our little mini-van packed up with supplies and facing outwards for a quick getaway if needed. A plan was put in place that involved evacuating the prison to Hautū Prison Farm on the other side of the mountain.

The role assigned to me in the event of an emergency evacuation was to ensure that all the prison records were buried in the bush outside the office. I knew what happened at Pompeii, so I had a sobering picture of archaeologists at some future time discovering the National Park site and speculating what this lone figure could possibly have been doing. Perhaps he had been digging his own grave when the lava solidified around him? This role for me was at variance with the arrangement for escape that Brenda and I had already agreed upon for our little family. Fortunately, the volcanic activity eventually subsided, and my loyalty to Queen, country and the Department of Justice was never tested.

Early in 1968 we received our passports back and were free to return to the UK if we wanted to. There had been times in the previous two years when we would have taken that option, had we been able to afford the fare, but now we knew New Zealand had much more to offer us as a family.

I saw out another year at Waikune before being appointed to a job in the head office of the Department of Justice in Wellington.

16

MOVING TO THE CAPITAL

We saw owning a house as the lynchpin for everything else we aspired to as a family. It was 1969, and people like us coming to Wellington could only afford to finance new houses in new subdivisions. So, three mortgages later, we walked into our new house in Wainuiomata. It was the last house on the road and sat on a completely bare section. The basic screwdriving skills I had learned from Uncle George at Barrington Road were not enough for me to lay concrete paths, erect fences, prepare lawns and all the other tasks that were the lot of a new suburban house owner in those days. Fortunately everyone was in the same situation and we all helped one another. I had little muscle and less skill to trade with our neighbours, but they seemed to tolerate me. I had to commute by bus and train for over two hours a day to work in the city. It seemed we had come across the world to end up in virtually the same situation we had left. The significant difference was that we now had Nick and Kay. In Wainuiomata there was a strong sense that everyone was in this together. Everyone was like us; young, broke and with children. It was suffocating. After only eighteen months, we realised we had made a mistake.

We moved out to rent a farmhouse at the back of Plimmerton before moving to Paekākāriki on the coast north of Wellington. That, too, was a long commute to work, but it offered the more established, heterogeneous community we were looking for. Right from the start of our marriage we had been desperate for security and normality, so it was ironic that we had already chalked up an average of two-plus houses for each year we had been married. I had a sense that we had at last found somewhere that suited us. Travelling home on the train from the city was a delight. At Pukerua Bay, the line is chipped into a high bank on the right, and to the left is the sea, with Kapiti Island a few kilometres away. Sometimes in summer, dolphins could be seen in the shimmering, still water. In winter the waves would swirl, smash against the rocks and spill onto the main road to the north that ran between the railway line and the sea. There were occasions, summer and winter, when I felt an indecent sense of wellbeing just to be coming home.

The Department of Justice in the early seventies managed prisons, courts, the probation service, land registry and a variety of subsidiary services and tribunals such as the Licensing Control Commission. In 1970 my first job was in the prisons branch, which was located in the main head office building at the end of Lambton Quay, opposite Parliament. The building was old, with uneven floors and peeling yellow paint. When the traffic outside was particularly heavy, the whole building would shiver as if preparing for an earthquake.

The office I was to work in looked like a dumping ground for files of various thickness and condition. Somewhere underneath the files were twenty or so battered wooden desks at which twenty or so men and women seemed to be diligently scribbling away or talking into dictaphones. I now knew what a pen-pusher looked like. Oh well, I thought, I have to start somewhere. Appearances were deceptive. What I was looking at was effectively the nerve centre of the country's prison system. I would play my part as the clearing house for a stream of queries coming in from prisons. These ranged from requests for home leave, to prison discipline issues, to a whole series of situations that arose in relation to the legislation. In addition I had my first experience of briefing a Minister and sometimes would draft speeches on matters relating to prisons. Everything was centralised then, and superintendents had very little autonomy. My experience at Waikune had taught me that things might be a little different in practice and that the more remote the institution, the more flexible superintendents were in interpreting head office dictates. By the time I got to Wellington, I had worked in prisons in the UK and New Zealand for six years and so I had good knowledge of how things happened. This helped me establish myself quite quickly in the new environment. Until then, I had seen my job as a routine one that just happened to be positioned in an odd environment. This changed as I began to see how some of the big decisions were made and concluded that, in some small way, I might be able to contribute to that.

The 1970s have been described as a golden era for the Department of Justice. John Robson was the Secretary for Justice, and Tom Shand had followed Ralph Hanan as the National government's Minister of Justice. Penal reform had been high on the government's agenda, although National did not have a good record in that respect. A National government had reintroduced capital punishment in 1950. Eleven years later Hanan, who was also the Minister at the time, was one of only ten National members who voted with Labour in a free vote in the House, which finally resulted in the limited abolition of capital punishment. If such a basic reform was so difficult to achieve then pushing anything else through was not going to be easy, particularly for a National government. Working away in the bowels of the department, I began to see a wider relevance for what I was doing. In 1972 the Kirk Labour government came in with another Minister of Justice, Martyn Finlay, and so reform remained on the agenda until 1975. From then, safer, more pragmatic approaches to the Justice portfolio were introduced by a series of ministers in Robert Muldoon's National government.

Further promotions saw me moved into other roles within the department. As Secretary of the Prisons Parole Board, I travelled to the main centres every six months. The board was chaired by a Supreme

Court judge and ensured that long-term prisoners, including those serving life imprisonment, were given a fair hearing in terms of the legislation. The board made decisions about possible release and pre-release arrangements. Other members of the board included Eric Missen, the new Secretary for Justice, a Dunedin magistrate, the Director of Mental Health and two government-appointed members. I was told that our arrival at institutions was usually a tense time for the local administration, particularly at Mt Eden and Pāremoremo, where most of the lifers were housed. I could see why. As far as some of the inmates were concerned, six anonymous men in suits arrived to interview and to make decisions about their future. In some cases the men (and occasionally a woman) had been waiting over a year since their last interview. Occasionally their anxiety infected the whole institution. Sometimes additional staff were brought in, just in case. This tension never seemed to spill over into the board hearings, which were generally quite calm affairs.

My role was purely administrative, but listening to the interaction between the board and the inmate and then sitting with the board while it continued its deliberations was instructive. It was privileged information in both senses of the word, but those discussions always seemed to me to be measured, compassionate and sensible. In those days the board's deliberations were closed to the media. The public, including the victims, were not kept informed about hearings and were not permitted to attend.

It was due to the nature of the slightly eccentric scope of activities of the Department of Justice at that time that I had some odd combinations of role. As well as being Secretary of the Prisons Parole Board, I managed some administrative aspects of the probation service, the prison service and was responsible also for managing the department's role with the Indecent Publications Tribunal.

Under the Indecent Publications Act 1963, the department was required to assess some material submitted by the members of the public, the Customs Department and the police. The assessment was carried out by one of the senior probation officers as an add-on to his normal role. How he got selected for the job was never quite clear to anyone, including him. Once he had done his assessment it was my job to ensure it was sent to the Minister with a suitable covering memorandum. It needs to be remembered that only a short time before, Mandy Rice-Davies, a model and star of the Profumo/Christine Keeler sex scandal in England, had been banned from entering the country as she was liable to 'deprave and corrupt' the populace. New Zealand also had some claim to fame around this time as being the country that had allowed the film *Ulysses* to be shown in cinemas, but only to audiences separated by gender.

Some of the memoranda that were sent to the Minister with alleged indecent material attached were little masterpieces in their own right. A typical response would look something like this:

I am attaching a copy of The Sex Act: An Instruction Manual which has been submitted by The Society for Promotion of Community Standards. Miss Bartlett has marked some illustrations and text which she believes to be indecent. We have examined the material and conclude that the book's claims to be instructive cannot be sustained. However, in our opinion, although titillating, The Sex Act: An Instruction Manual is not indecent in terms of the Act and should not be referred to the Indecent Publications Tribunal. I am attaching a letter to Miss Bartlett for your signature if you agree.

I was later to find out what happened when this material was received in the Minister's office. I was temporarily assigned there as a ministerial secretary a few times during a particularly somnolent period of the National government in the mid-1970s. The Minister of Justice at the time was not known for his interest in the reforming aspects of his portfolio. However, he did have other interests. I was there one Friday afternoon, incredibly pleased with myself at having made it to such a hallowed place with such an important title, but I was rather bored as there was nothing much to do. The Minister came into my office, briefcase in hand.

"Anything for my weekend, Peter?" he asked, nodding towards my tray marked *For Minister's Signature.*

"There's a report on release to work parole, some JP appointments, the draft Annual Report, or there are these for the tribunal," I said, pulling out some shiny magazines and a book with exotic and provocative titles clipped behind a sober covering memorandum from the department.

"I think I'll just take these," he said, lifting the tribunal material into his briefcase. He didn't smile. Nor did I.

At Paekākāriki, Kay and Nick were off to the local school and Brenda was working and studying for her science degree. We began to feel we had passed some sort of probationary period and were now *bona fide* parents. As a family we were getting on well, and there seemed to be plenty of warmth and laughter among us all in the house.

I had written to Shaw when we got to Wellington from National Park, thanking him for what he had done for me and for Mum over the years. I received a brief, warm note in reply, together with a cheque for fifty pounds. I never heard from him again apart from a card each year at Christmas time. Shaw died in 1976. I was later to learn that he had met my father just a few months beforehand.

When I had left Heathrow on that grey freezing day in December 1965, I was not expecting that I would ever return. So it was surprising that, twelve years later, we somehow found the means for the family to fly to the UK for a visit. We had an overwhelming urge to return before we finally committed to New Zealand, but it was more than that. Some friends had found they were unable to keep solemn promises to maintain contact after we left for New Zealand. We had tired of trying to engage with them at distance as correspondence trickled down to the odd postcard and a desultory card at Christmas time. Two or three had conscientiously kept in touch and had not allowed distance to interfere with the friendship. In the absence of close family, it was those friends who became vitally important to us as we adjusted to a new country. We needed to let them know what they meant to us.

There was a lot that was familiar in England. It was good to be able to show the children the reality of Monopoly board London, visit the soft undulating Kent countryside, and stand outside places that had existed before Māori had set foot in New Zealand. Of Mum's sisters, Hilda and May had left Ilford for retirement living in Norfolk, but Agnes was still in the East End and was still confused about what was going on around her. All their lives seemed to me to have been predestined. I was beginning to understand why Mum had decided so early in life to take a different path from that of her sisters.

I visited Phyllis at Red Hill, and she told me what little she knew about my father. I felt very disconnected from Red Hill. The last time I had been there was for Mum's funeral, and my feeling of alienation and indifference towards my father had remained since that time. He could have got in touch in the intervening years but had chosen not to do so. I was not ready to risk rejection, although it would have been easy enough to find him while we were there.

Phyllis seemed dispirited. With Shaw gone she had lost her inspiration. Shaw, like many charismatic leaders, had been reluctant, or unable, to foster similar charisma amongst his likely successors. Phyllis felt the future for the school was beginning to look bleak, particularly as some of the innovations Shaw introduced at Red Hill were being adopted by mainstream institutions as the education system freed up.

Brenda and I waited for the pull of the motherland while we were there, but it did not come. We were glad to sink back into the Air New Zealand connecting flight to Auckland and listen to the familiar New Zealand accents around us. We were happy to be returning home.

Apart from the period with the Kent County Library, all my working life had been spent in the justice sector, mostly in operational positions of some sort. In 1979 I began a series of moves that took me from the Department of Justice to policy work in the Department of Social Welfare and change management positions in the National Library and the Tourist and Publicity Department.

I did wonder whether I had the visionary thinking that was going to be required for policy work. I needn't have worried. From what I could see, there was always tension between social policy and political expediency, with departments like Social Welfare caught between the two. I often found myself moved to projects designed to meet short-term crises. Some of these projects had doubtful merit. An example was my appointment in 1980 to the working party on Community Services and Youth. The Returned and Services Association (RSA) had been lobbying strongly for a form of compulsory military training. An earlier version had been abandoned in the 1960s. The aim of the new proposal was to address the problems of antisocial behaviour amongst the young by compelling all young people to participate in military-style training and participation in community and welfare activity. The RSA idea was prompted by what it saw as concerns that:

The three Vs present a growing threat to our future – violence, vandalism and venereal disease taken together with or possibly as a consequence of the recent positive and alarming increase in drug use, seem to us to present as great a social problem as the people of this country have had to face in recent years.

The incoming National government agreed to set up a working party of officials. I was to represent the Department of Social Welfare on the working party. There were fourteen other officials, including one from Prime Minister Robert Muldoon's office presumably there to keep an eye on us. We sat through months of deliberation, including a solemn analysis of what became known as 'the three Vs'. I doubt the politicians were surprised at the outcome when the report was presented in 1982. We concluded that compelling all young people to go into community service simply to address the problems of the relatively few who were at risk, could not be justified. The report was quietly shelved, but the subject has often surfaced in one form or another at general elections since then.

By the time I got to the Tourist and Publicity Department, major changes were sweeping through the public sector, culminating in the election of the Lange Labour government in 1984. 'Corporatisation', 'market forces' and 'redundancy' became new words to get used to. Some public sector managers took the opportunity to leave; others kept their heads down and hoped it would all go away. For me, some of what was being proposed began to make a lot of sense, particularly at the Tourist and Publicity Department. What, for instance, was the government doing operating travel agencies and a major park complex in Rotorua like some Intourist operation in East Europe? I became embroiled in the change process and in doing so cashed in some of the more extreme of the socialist values that had been instilled in me during those early years when Shaw had been running for parliament. If I was shifting slightly from the left, it was nothing compared to the shift to the right of the Labour government of the time, which was bent on an economic agenda of which Margaret Thatcher would have been proud.

Meanwhile, in Paekākāriki, the door that had closed softly behind Brenda and I when we married now seemed to both of us to be bolted from the outside. We recognised that immigration to New Zealand, particularly to National Park, had deepened the love we felt for one another. This had carried through to our new life in Wellington, but gradually we were finding our own way: she through her interests in science and the work she was doing with the DSIR, and me in senior change management roles I had never expected to attain. We no longer depended upon one another in the way we had and, without that, we gradually drifted apart. We talked about separation, but neither of us had the courage to make the final move, mainly because of the impact on the children and the family life we had created.

Finally, in 1982, Brenda decided she wanted to move out and live on her own. I felt admiration for her more than resentment. We again discussed how this might affect the children. There is never a completely right way of dealing with these situations. Presenting Kay and Nick with a *fait accompli* seemed to us the only alternative. We thought, correctly, that Nick might not be too surprised. He was leaving school and was already developing his own way of dealing with life events. He has since said he was uneasy that the parents he thought coped so well suddenly seemed so unsure of themselves. We worried that all this would be more of a shock to Kay, and so it proved. She was upset but reassured that Brenda and I were still genuinely friends and nobody else was involved. It also helped that I would be staying with both children in the house in Paekākāriki. I remained there as a solo father to two teenage children for a year or so.

We eventually sold the Paekākāriki house, and Nick and I ended up flatting together. Kay went to live with Brenda, finishing sixth form and going on to get her zoology degree. Nick and I flatting together in central Wellington while he was on the journalism course at polytech was not quite the fun time we had anticipated. I seemed to be constantly opening the door to his visitors. I would watch in surprise, and perhaps a little envy, as some beautiful young vision would be ushered down to his dark and chaotic room. I did not know what to do with my own life as a single person. Although work was going well, I was confused and restless, still wanting freedoms whilst craving domesticity. This was a dangerous place to be, as many men in late middle age can testify.

In 1987, full of self-confidence and a new-found ambition, I took a step too far. I was appointed as a director at the Department of Inland Revenue. IRD had managed to avoid the major thrusts of public sector reform. I had some idea from my experience with restructuring in the Tourist and Publicity Department that strategic and operational change at IRD was as desirable as it was inevitable, but I knew it would be difficult to manage in such a monolithic organisation with the Commissioner edging towards retirement and not wanting to change too much on his watch. It did not help that I was the only director in the senior team at the time who did not have a tax background and a long history in the department. To its credit, IRD had overseen the introduction of the new goods and Services Tax (GST). Maybe as a result of that success, there was a sense of complacency around the organisation; a feeling that it was somehow a protected species as far as public sector change was concerned.

There were occasional havens of relaxation and laughter. Towards the end of my time at IRD, a group of us involved in managing the change used to meet in my office for Friday drinks after work. The laughter could be a little hysterical at times, but many of us were working up to fifteen hour days, six days per week. Sue Christie had moved up to Wellington from Christchurch to work on a change project. I remembered her from an earlier visit I had made to Christchurch. I had been clearing up after a meeting and talking to one or two people when a slight figure pushed through the group to stand in front of me. She was an attractive woman in her forties, impeccably dressed with blonde/white hair. "Are you the Peter Farrell who's been sending out all that information about what's going on?" She spoke clearly and directly. I nodded warily. The Christchurch office was known to be suspicious of change in any form, particularly if the messenger was not 'one of us'. The response to my visit that day had generally been very negative. "I thought you were. I just wanted to say thank you for what you are doing. That's never happened here before. It's really good information," she said, before quickly turning and leaving. I lost sight of her as she disappeared into the crowd. It was rare that anyone indicated to me that the work I was doing was anything other than a threat and a hindrance to them, so that brief speech was something to treasure.

"Who was that?" I said, turning to one of the group who was looking after me.

"That's Sue Christie. She hasn't been here long." I knew that could mean that she had arrived in the last five years or so. "She used to be a full-time union organiser for the Public Service Association in Christchurch," he said disparagingly. The inference was clear. She was trouble and needed keeping an eye on.

Sometime later, Sue's name came up again, applying to work on one of the projects we were setting up in Wellington. "That's the woman who said thank you," I said, recognising the name immediately. "We need someone like that here!"

Far from being trouble, Sue brought a clear enquiring mind and an incredible work ethic. More than that, her ability to laugh at herself and with others around her was infectious. I found myself missing her presence when she did not turn up to Friday drinks.

Progress was slow getting IRD to at least recognise some fundamental improvements were needed in the organisation to meet what was going to be required of it by the government. It was a bit like hanging on to the helm of a huge ocean liner; the wheel had been turned a whole revolution, but the bow of the vessel had shifted only infinitesimally towards safety.

Fortunately, a new Commissioner was appointed who was very determined to lead the change required. This was a help. For me, it was too late. Although the work was more focused, workloads increased along with the pressure to deliver results as well as manage the administration of one of the largest government departments in the country. I recognised I was becoming overwhelmed, exhausted and in danger of complete collapse. Following the public sector reforms of the eighties, my guidance had sometimes been sought from others who had found they were not coping. My advice was always the same. To hell with ambition. Look after yourself, and find somewhere you can start again. After just over two years in the job, it was time to listen to my own advice. I resigned.

IRD might have put paid to my ambitions to further progress through the ranks, but it was not an unmitigated disaster for me. I had been involved at the start of some significant changes, and it was at IRD where I first met Sue Christie.

Just before I left the organisation, she had moved to a more permanent position in Wellington. It seemed natural we would continue to see one another once she had settled in. In a restaurant one evening she talked about her childhood in Rangiora. She described packing the Austin 7 for family holidays at Waikuku Beach and spending time at the swimming pool in the summer. Her aunt was the local mayoress, and her grandmother and other family members all lived nearby. She was still in touch with school friends whom she had met at primary school. She said she had had an idyllic New Zealand childhood. It certainly sounded like it to me. I tried to explain Red Hill to her and why I thought my own childhood was also idyllic, but in a different way. Sitting in a Wellington restaurant, forty or so years later and twelve thousand miles removed, a Red Hill childhood was a difficult concept for me to describe or for her to completely understand.

She said that, regardless of her idyllic childhood, she grew into a bolshie teenager. "I used to dye my hair bright red, wear beatle boots and a miniskirt covering very little," she smiled, fiddling with her wine glass. "My poor dad must have despaired of me."

I thought about the difference in our ages. "You know I am only four years older than you, but for all that background at Red Hill, there is no way I would have rebelled in the way you did." I didn't tell her that night but I thought the teenage Sue would have scared me to death.

We found we'd had similar experiences in the central North Island. While I was at Waikune as a new immigrant, Sue was living with her first husband who worked in forestry in Kāingaroa Forest near Rotorua.

"I found that life really hard, and unlike you, I didn't have to cope with being in a new country," she said sympathetically. "I can't believe that no one took you in over that first Christmas." I had already seen plenty of evidence that her extrovert exterior hid an extraordinary care for others, something I had not come across to that degree in anyone else I knew. Kāingaroa had been a difficult time, as her marriage collapsed around her and she was faced with the tragic loss of her young daughter who had died of leukaemia.

Sue had a collection of war stories from her time in the union. She said that when she had started as an organiser she had been surprised at how much anxiety could be engendered in employers' minds just by her appearance at a workplace.

"A smart mouth and a bit of status bought a lot of power in those days," she told me. I smiled. I'd had my problems with union organisers over the years. I would not have wanted to face Sue across the table.

Surely there would be something to make me uneasy, something to make me close off and withdraw. Much to my delight, I found my admiration for her was returned in equal measure. Admiration, staying together, living together and love all tumbled one after another in quick succession.

17

A NEW START

After finishing at IRD in 1989, I resolved to pull back and start again. The National Art Gallery and National Museum coexisted in the same building on Buckle Street in Wellington as branches of the Department of Internal Affairs. There were plans to amalgamate the two under one Board and one Chief Executive and set them up as one independent institution, separate from the Department of Internal Affairs. This looked like a similar situation to the one I had faced at the National Library a few years earlier. I was appointed to take charge of the people side of the operation at the National Art Gallery and Museum as a first step to amalgamation. This later expanded to a wider role as a director reporting to the Chief Executive, but initially I wanted to take stock. I enjoyed work, and I had become good at what I did. I just needed to recover my confidence. This was a good place to start.

Fortunately things were quiet at the beginning, so I had time to try and make sense of the organisation I had joined. The National Art Gallery had its own board and director, as did the National Museum. They operated quite separately, mostly in the same building with some shared services like security. The New Zealand Academy of Fine Arts also occupied gallery and office space in the building. The Academy, too, had its own governance arrangement. The National Gallery and Museum directors had some autonomy over collections but very little else. As far as I could see, wherever you started in the power game, sooner or later you would end up with the Department of Internal Affairs who held all the cards. In 1989 the department had a whole host of functions. It seemed to treat the museum and the art gallery as it would cleaning services, war graves, community development or any other member of its far-flung empire. They were, in the parlance of the day, simply cost centres.

The imposing Dominion Museum building had opened in Wellington in 1936. Wellington did not expand in quite the direction anticipated, and the Buckle Street location became quite isolated from the city. It did not help that the department had allowed the building to deteriorate through lack of maintenance. It was also an earthquake risk, as were the other buildings occupied by the museum dotted around the city. Research activity seemed to be well respected in the communities of interest that it served, but attracting people to Buckle Street to visit their museum became increasingly difficult. There were occasionally very successful one-off exhibitions like Te Māori and exhibitions from other overseas art collections. Otherwise, it was frequently the case that security staff would outnumber visitors in the cavernous galleries, particularly on weekdays.

The government set up a project board headed by ex-Prime Minister Bill Rowling to plan for a new museum on the Wellington waterfront. In 1992 legislation was enacted setting up the Museum of New Zealand Te Papa Tongarewa – Te Papa. The concept for the new museum was controversial. Most seemed to agree with removing the activities from the Department of Internal Affairs, but combining the National Art Gallery and the National Museum under one board and one chief executive did not meet with universal approval. The fine arts community to this day continues to lobby for a separate national art gallery. The building design was also the subject of great debate within the media.

Once funding was approved and the legislation passed, the pressures from outside began to build. Te Papa was an expensive undertaking by New Zealand standards and there was some expectation that it would be a spectacular failure.

It was an immense project involving the building of the new museum and developing the programmes, activities and exhibitions to the highest possible specifications. The project team responsible for that work and bringing in the project on time and on budget was made up from some of the most talented people in their fields. I learned a lot just watching them at work.

Part of my role was to oversee the organisational change that would be required for the museum to operate in a different way at the new location. I was aware of the debate surrounding the concept and the building, but most of us involved at the time felt we had a brief and a job to do so we needed to get on and do it. However, there were occasions when the task seemed so overwhelming and the opposition from some quarters so remorseless that I contemplated leaving. I am glad I didn't.

Many of the academic/curatorial and conservation staff in both the museum and the art gallery were gifted experts in their own disciplines and used to a stable environment. They liked the prospect of moving from under the yoke of the Department of Internal Affairs but were anxious about what might replace it. Academic disciplines tended to keep to themselves and there was no contact at all between the art group on one side and the scientists and historians on the other. At one meeting I remember introducing two curators who had worked in the same building for over twenty years. Although the Te Māori exhibition had been an outstanding success both here and overseas, there was little evidence of much of a shift in attitudes towards Māori culture and taonga and how they should be treated. The attention the new museum was to give to the place of Māori was another area for controversy.

The establishment of a position of Kaihautū, which sat alongside the Chief Executive raised a few eyebrows. Te Papa was fortunate in that the first appointee to this position was Cliff Whiting of Te Whānau-ā-Apanui, a Māori carver and teacher with a huge reputation. Cliff's contribution can be seen in the marae at Te Papa, which was itself a major building project among a building project. Cliff's use of contemporary material and methods caused much debate among Māori and elsewhere in the community. His quiet influence ran deeply through the culture of the place, and through him, many of us began to understand exactly what a bicultural institution might look like. That same influence impacted on me on a personal level, as it was Cliff who first talked to me about the meaning of 'whānau' or extended family.

The Te Papa board, management team and staff were given a demanding brief by the government. The founding Chief Executive, Cheryll Sotheran was, in my observation, visionary and focused. Without her, it is doubtful the project would have been completed as successfully as it was. However, there were costs to the counter-productive style of leadership she employed, and I sometimes found myself ministering to bruised and broken egos, casualties of the frenetic drive to get the job done.

An objective account of the establishment of Te Tapa on the Wellington waterfront has still to be written. For me, the Te Papa environment at that time was innovative, eccentric, sometimes anarchic, often controversial but ultimately successful – a description that could also be used to describe Red Hill School under Otto Shaw where I spent the first seventeen years of my life.

It was a clear bright day when Te Papa opened on the Wellington waterfront on 14 February 1998. Waka were in the harbour, and huge queues of people crowded the forecourt, waiting patiently to see their new museum. On that first day, thirty thousand people went through and within six months of opening, 1.3 million had visited, with ninety-seven percent of those indicating they would return. There was pride and excitement amongst all of us involved in whatever role we had played in getting the project completed. Elaine Guerian was an advisor/mentor to the Te Papa Project for a number of years. She had been Assistant Secretary at the Smithsonian in Washington and had led a number of high-profile museum projects in America including the Boston Children's Museum and the Holocaust Museum in Washington. She sought me out on opening day. "Not many people know it," she said quietly, "but I do. I see your fingerprints behind the scenes all over this place." Coming from her, that was recognition indeed. I remembered the time of my arrival there in 1989 when I thought my career was at an end. I was glad I had come, and I was glad I had seen the project through.

I had Cliff Whiting and others to thank for my exposure to Māori concepts over the previous nine years. Some of those concepts remain a mystery to me. However, I did come to understand what Māori mean by whānau, extended family, and how indestructible it was. I was not brought up in a family, and I struggled as a parent, but that did not mean I didn't have whānau who were there for me as I was for them.

My childhood may have been unusual, but it was very happy.

Bike riding around the grounds at Red Hill, 1950.

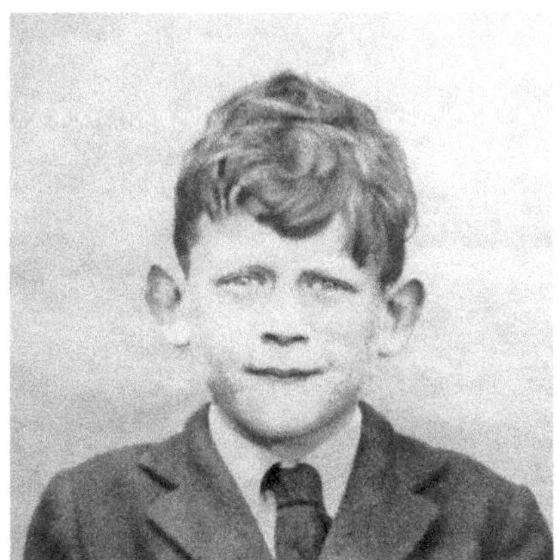

Primary school 'mug shot' taken at Sutton Valence in 1946.

Mum with me and my cousin Sheila at Red Hill in 1942.

A print of Eruera Patuone, Rangatira of the Ngāpuhi iwi of New Zealand hung in my small room at Red Hill, which I shared with another boy during the war. I never did find out why Mum found the man so interesting.
Photo: Auckland Art Gallery Toi o Ta̅maki, gift of Mr H F. Partridge, 1915.

Red Hill boys at a camp on the school estate. I am sitting in front at far right. The adult is Colin Hart, the school cook, 1946/47.

Mum beginning to show some of the strains of life. *Photo by Red Hill boy Clifford Ling, 1946/7.*

Marion with Pamela Adam who left Red Hill in 1947 when the school was closed to girls.

Mum and me outside the Upper Cottage, 1954/5.

Marion was nicknamed MOF by the Red Hill boys. She was used to sitting through endless meetings, debating issues in her forthright way.

The Red Hill Court was held in the impressive wood-panelled dining room. I loved sitting in there listening to the dramas, but I did not take an active part.

Ralph Grigglestone and me in 1946. Ralph did not get on with Shaw, so Marion took him under her wing and Ralph looked after me.

Off to Eltham College in 1952. I often wonder how I managed being a public schoolboy and then coming home to Red Hill in the holidays.

1958 and about to start my first job at Kent County Library. I never really understood what librarians were supposed to do, although Mr Gen the barber did have some advice for me.

Phyllis Oliver along with my mother and one or two others held Red Hill together during the post-war years. Phyllis was the keeper of many secrets and remains a dear friend.

Mum as I remember her 1955. I kept this photo with me when I went away to school.

The Liverpool Blue Coat School in the late 50s provided a flexible, innovative environment for boarders and day boys.

Brenda and I married in 1962.

Holloway Prison, London. Going to work there meant entering a different world every morning. *Photo: Getty Images.*

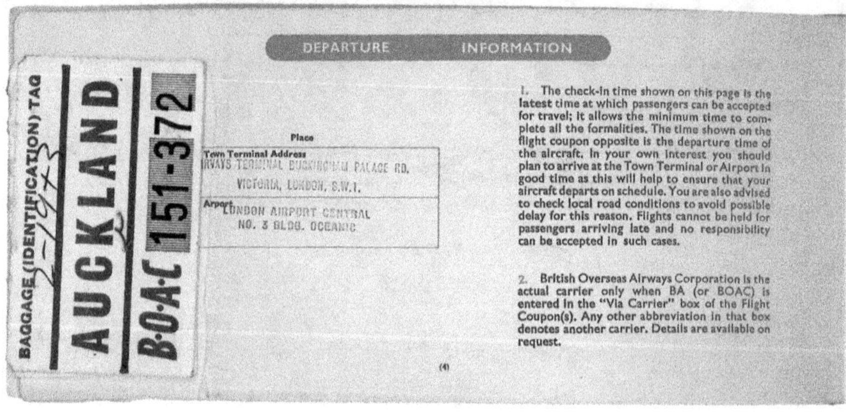

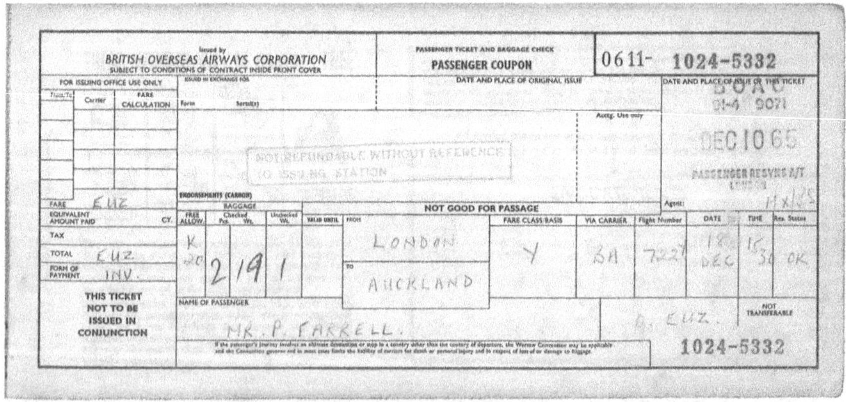

I had never been to an airport, let alone flown in a plane, and here was the New Zealand Government offering to pay our fares. I was later to find out why.

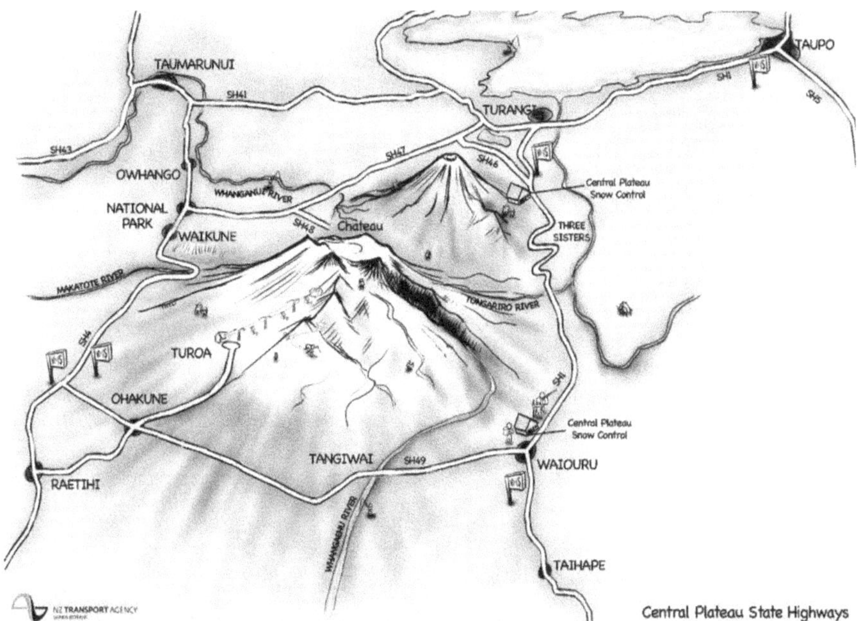

There were few escapes from Waikune. Not many inmates were prepared to take on the inhospitable landscape.

National Park Station in June 2013. Not much has changed since I arrived there in December 1965.

I could see Mount Ngāuruhoe etched clearly against the skyline when I arrived at National Park in December 1965. *Photo: Chris and Jo Sollom.*

My room in the single officers' quarters was comfortable enough. I was used to institutional living. *Photo: New Zealand Corrections Department.*

Waikune Prison looked rather like a large unkempt motel. *Photo: New Zealand Corrections Department.*

Cliff Whiting (Kaihautū) Ken Gorbey (Director), me, Graeme Shadbolt (Director) at Te Papa site, 1997.

Me on opening day, 14 February 1998.

With Sue and new beginnings.

The Farrells are reunited for a celebration. Kay, me, Brenda and Nick. Kay now lives in Abu Dhabi and Nick in Rome.

PART 3
DISCOVERY

18

THE SEARCH BEGINS

Why then? Why 1994 and not earlier? I had for years had all the information I needed to find my father, so why had it taken until then for me to do something about it?

Sue and I were on holiday in the Cook Islands in 1994 when it occurred to me that, for the first time ever, everything in my life was settled and happy. Our new life together was working well; my children were adult and showing initiatives of their own; funding for Te Papa had been approved and the prospect of on-going stimulating work there looked promising. In my working environment, I was forever hearing about the critical importance of family and whānau. At Te Papa, Cliff Whiting and some other Māori on the staff talked to me about my background and were baffled that I could be so disinterested in my origins.

I had never felt the absence of a father in my life, although I did struggle to understand how families worked. Mum had done a good job as a parent, and Red Hill had provided me with plenty of stimulating male company. I had always believed that it was she, rather than me, who was the victim of the story that was fabricated around my birth. As I grew older I became aware that I may have been harbouring anger against my father for longer than I cared to admit. I had no expectations of reconciliation, but I did want to know more about his relationship with Mum and why he had turned away from me so completely, particularly after she died.

In 1994 I felt entirely safe; safe enough to look for my father. I was ready to handle rejection if that was to be the outcome.

I knew from Mum, during that uncomfortable conversation years previously, that my father's name was Morris Horovitch. I had kept in touch with Phyllis Oliver, Shaw's secretary, over the years. Shaw had kept his promise not to pass on the secret to anyone, but he underestimated Phyllis's perception. She had told me she once accompanied Shaw to a meeting of the Association of Workers for Maladjusted Children, at which Morris Horovitch was speaking. As soon as she saw him, she had said to Shaw, "That's Peter Farrell's father, isn't it?" I must have been about ten at that time. Phyllis was the keeper of many secrets of Red Hill, and this became just another one. She never volunteered any information to me, as she said that I had not seemed interested in my father whenever the question was raised. She noticed a change as my own children grew up and I began to seek some basic details.

Phyllis was a great friend and supporter of my mother and seemed interested in what I was up to in New Zealand. It was Phyllis who told me that Morris had another son, David, whom she thought was an actor. Phyllis also thought there may have been a daughter.

When we got back from the Cook Islands, I commenced the search for my father. I already had Mum's poems, and there were one or two letters she had kept for me to find. I now knew through Phyllis it was possible that my half-brother was an actor, although the name David Horovitch was not familiar to me. This was before the age of the internet, but I thought I would be able to find something about him at the Wellington Public Library. I found an Actors' Directory in the reference section. I turned to the letter H, and there he was, slotted somewhere in between Anthony Hopkins and Bob Hoskins. There was a photograph, and so I borrowed a magnifying glass from the reference librarian. I bent closer to examine every detail of the black and white image in front of me. There were some similarities with the face. There was something about the eyes, the posture and the hairline, but what was more surprising was that the face was familiar to me for other reasons. It was the face of one of those English actors who appear regularly on television but whose name you never quite remember. I realised I had watched him often over the years in such series as *The Bill, Bognor, Miss Marple* and *A Piece of Cake.*

The directory showed his year of birth as 1945, five years after mine. It looked as though he had gone straight from school to the Central School of Drama in fashionable Hampstead in North London, one of the leading schools for actors. He seemed to have embarked upon his acting career from there. He had been successful on the stage, television and in one or two films. His hobbies were shown as walking and cricket. Very English, I thought. I noticed he had stuck with the Jewish name and the rather unusual spelling. There was mention of a father and mother, both teachers. There was also a wife (divorced), children and an elder sister.

There was no mention of a brother.

I rang work and said I wouldn't be in that afternoon. I photocopied the extract from the directory, including my brother's photograph, folded it carefully in my briefcase and made for Roy Parsons bookshop on Lambton Quay. They made good coffee there and it was usually reasonably quiet. I needed a place to think and to look at David's picture again. Roy Parsons had recently expanded its collection of videos, and just by the stairs up to the café, I noticed there was a shelf containing the full BBC series of *Miss Marple*. I knew from the directory extract I had in my briefcase that David Horovitch had played Inspector Slack in that series. I chose *The Mirror Cracked.* It was a murder mystery set in a school.

I was home early that night but tried to keep myself occupied waiting for Sue to arrive. Eventually I heard the key in the lock and rushed to her like a child at Christmas. I spread out the photocopy of the directory as if it was some piece of homework of which I was particularly proud.

"Wow. I didn't think we'd find anything that quickly." I was grateful for the 'we'. "I don't want to watch a video tonight," she said, noticing what was in my hand. "I don't think I could concentrate with all this going on."

"I think you will want to watch *this* video." I showed her David's name on the cast list.

Everything else was forgotten as I slotted the video cassette into the player. The screen flickered and then settled. The credits played over a backdrop of 1940s English home counties. I shivered slightly and leant forward, searching for the name. It was the last to appear.

Also starring as Inspector Slack – David Horovitch.

It was twenty minutes into the story and still no Inspector Slack. My finger hovered over the fast forward button. After a lifetime being at the beck and call of others, I was suddenly able to move time forward to my own agenda.

"Be patient. It can't be long," Sue whispered, her voice tense, and then, "God, look at *that*!"

On the screen, Inspector Slack had made his entrance. He was doing a bit of business with a top hat, something to do with a penchant for magic. That was irrelevant. The long forehead, thinning hair and quizzical eyebrows were features I saw in the mirror most mornings. The hat dropped away from his face, revealing the full profile. I swallowed deeply, waiting for him to move and to speak. Inspector Slack eventually spoke, in the flat vowels of Essex, so there were no more clues there. However, when he moved there were some things the actor could not disguise. He was taller than me, sure, but there was that slight stoop years of training had not quite edited out.

We ran and reran the video, halting it every time Inspector Slack appeared. David would never before have had an acting performance of his so closely analysed. It seemed to me it was unlikely he knew of my existence at that time, but I could not be sure.

Finding my father's address and telephone number was a relatively easy next step. I decided to ring him at the number in Shenfield, Essex, just out of London. I set the alarm for 5.00am one morning, knowing it would be 4.00pm in the evening of the previous day in England, a good time to be ringing someone approaching ninety years old, I thought. I dialled the code for the UK and started to dial the number. I hesitated on the last digit, then slipped the phone back in its cradle. I was only going to get one chance at this. I needed to think of exactly what I was going to say to him and give him time to consider how he should respond. So I decided I would write instead.

The letter I sent him on 28 December 1994 took hours to draft. I knew that Shaw had kept Morris in touch with my progress until 1976, so he would be aware I was in New Zealand. That was the first hurdle dealt with. Morris would be unlikely to see me as an immediate threat from that distance. I tried to put myself in his shoes. He may have felt guilt and apprehension that this letter that he may have been half expecting over the years had finally arrived. Alternatively, he would have known that I was fifty-four, and so may have thought I had moved on. I had to reassure him I was not after anything from him but reconciliation and understanding. There was also the question of his wife and children and whether or not they knew about his affair with Marion. If they didn't know, how would he want to protect them? I had calculated he would be well into his eighties by then so might be ready to acknowledge me. I almost, but not quite, felt sorry for him having to deal with this after all the years that had passed.

I had no expectations he would reply. That was one of the reasons for waiting this long. I was ready, almost expecting, rejection. If I had a hope, rather than an expectation, it was that, through him, I might get to know my mother better. I enclosed some photographs of me, as I knew from the photographs and video I had seen of David, that there was no doubting that I was Morris's son. I added some photos of Kay and Nick, just to remind him of another generation that existed.

I had decided to handwrite the letter. As well as checking and rechecking the content for me, Sue had to check my writing was sufficiently legible for elderly eyes. Whatever I was initiating could impact upon both Sue and me. We talked again and speculated about possible outcomes. She had waited some time for me to get to this stage. She had said, if my father's address had been available when she was last in London on her own, she could well have gone down to Shenfield to see if she could sight him. We laughed at the image of her knocking on his door and then running off as soon as he appeared. She was relieved I was finally making this move and just as excited and fearful as me at what might happen next. We decided if there was no reply to the letter, I would telephone him. If that didn't elicit a response, there was always my half-brother David. He should be easy enough to contact.

I entered Morris's Shenfield address on the envelope and sealed it. I decided not to put a sender's address on the outside. The stamp and the postmark would be enough, whereas a sender's address may give him away if he had not told his wife. The mid-summer sun was warm on my back when I slipped the envelope into the box at the Kilbirnie Post Office in Wellington.

Mary, Morris's wife, was the only person apart from Shaw who he had entrusted with his secret. Two weeks later an airmail letter postmarked London arrived in our letterbox in Alexandra Road, at the top of Mount Victoria in Wellington.

My letter had not been a complete surprise for Mary as she knew I had gone to New Zealand, but she had some news for me.

I have to tell you that he died on 15 July 1994 of a heart attack. How sad your letter came only a few months too late, she had written, in a precise careful tone that was to become so familiar.

Mary had also enclosed a photograph of her and Morris taken just before he died. I turned the photograph over in my hand, examining it closely, waiting to feel some connection with the image before me.

"I know what you're going to look like when you are eighty," Sue said, looking over my shoulder.

I couldn't see the likeness, although there was something about the set of his head that was perhaps familiar. Otherwise, to me, he just looked like an old man sitting with his wife on a park bench.

Now he was dead. It must have happened about that time in the Cook Islands when I decided to start looking for him. I searched myself for some sense of loss but could find none. The man in the photograph had not been a living person to me. I had edited him out of my life in much the same way he had deleted me from his. I doubted I would ever learn about the relationship he had with my mother. Yet perhaps these other people on the other side of the world could help me know the sort of man my father was, and from that, I might understand more about my mother.

In a strange way, Morris's death caused me once more to grieve for Mum and mourn my inability to establish an adult relationship with her. Mum had been at least three people during her life: Marion in her early life; MOF at Red Hill; and she had always been Mum to me. It was the Marion that Morris knew who, with his death, would now probably be lost to me forever.

19

MEETING THE WHĀNAU

Morris's wife Mary said in her letter she would try and tell me anything I wanted to know about my father. She had a caveat. *I have a daughter and a son. I hope you will not mind if I ask that you do <u>not</u> seek them out. Morris never told them about you and I know it was his wish they should not know.* She was too late. I had traced my brother and was confident it would not take much to find his sister. I knew they were my half-brother and half-sister but I had already made up my mind they would be my brother and sister, unless they wished it otherwise. I would find them both if I had to.

Mary was a product of her generation and it was understandable she wanted to protect her husband's reputation. The search had taken years to get under way. Now, the speed of events was disconcerting, but I was not going to let the matter rest there. I wrote another letter, carefully asking her to reconsider, pointing out that the children must be into middle age and capable of making up their own minds. I also sent more photographs of myself just in case she had any lingering concerns about the validity of the relationship. To her great credit she replied quickly, saying, *I have decided to tell the children — 'children' no longer. Gillian is*

51 and David 49. They are coming here on Sunday. I will tell them then.

My half-brother and sister were summoned to the family home in Shenfield. It was just three months after Sue and I had so minutely analysed David's performance in *Miss Marple*. They have since told me that, on the drive from London, they speculated on the reason for the summons. They had seen Mary regularly since their father's funeral six months previously and had not noticed anything particularly unusual to warrant such an urgent call from their mother. They assumed it was something to do with their father, perhaps an issue about the estate. They later gave me an account of what happened.

My understanding was that Mary was waiting for them when they came in. "I have something to tell you. Do you want me to do that now or shall we have a cup of tea first?" She seemed more than usually preoccupied.

"I think you'd better tell us now, Mum." They were beginning to feel some apprehension. My letter to Morris and the later ones to her, together with the photographs, were lying on the table in front of them.

"Well, I think I'll go and make a cup of tea anyway. Look through those while I'm in the kitchen," she said, indicating the papers on the table. "We'll talk when you have seen them." She seemed relieved to leave them to it.

David didn't bother with the letters. He eagerly reached for one of the photographs and looked at it carefully. It was obvious. "I think we have a brother," he said, looking at Gill.

In her next letter, after the visit, Mary reported, *I have told Gillian and David and they have taken it very well and are actually delighted.* She was still firm in her view that the wider family should not be told. She had already told me about my paternal grandparents Hymie and Sophie, who had immigrated to London from Europe in 1900. Yiddish was spoken in the family, and Morris was the first person in the family to be proficient in written and spoken English. She described her own background as middle class; *my father was an architect and my mother was a snob.* If she wanted to keep both branches of the wider family ignorant of my existence, that was okay by me. She seemed to enjoy writing to me. Once she had had the meeting with Gill and David, long letters arrived every week or so from her. It was from these and my later conversations with her I was able to gain some insights into my father's life and personality. Only when she wrote about meeting and eventually marrying Morris did I sense she was very carefully considering the implication of her words. She wrote of meeting Mum when she and Morris visited Red Hill soon after I had been born. I thought I detected a hint of condescension in her description of that occasion. However if I wanted to proceed with my search, I would have to be careful not to be oversensitive or overprotective unless I, too, tried to reinvent the past to protect reputations.

Within a very few days, two letters with London postmarks arrived for me. One was from David and the other from Gill. David's letter expanded upon what I had already found out about him from my research in the library. He was obviously a well-established working actor who seemed quietly proud of his achievements. He was currently appearing in the West End as Prince Philip in *The Queen and I*, but there was a whole string of theatre, radio and television credits to his name, including Inspector Slack. He wrote that he had been described recently as a 'successful actor', *so I suppose it must be true but I think that success is something perceived from the outside rather than experienced from the inside.* He was divorced, with two boys still at home: Tom who was studying law and Francis who was studying music with plans to teach or perform. David made no mention of a partner.

Gill said she had qualified as a nurse but later switched to social work, gaining a master's degree in her forties. She wrote about Morris getting his master's degree in his eighties and sent some newspaper cuttings about that. Her husband, John, was also a social worker. They had two children. She said Nathan and Gemma had both been fascinated to learn they had a new uncle and two new cousins. Gill also included some material that had been read out at Morris's funeral a few months earlier.

Both letters were welcoming and open. They were followed up with a number of phone calls that, for me anyway, were surprisingly easy. In one of these calls, Gill said she would have to reconcile herself to abdicating from her role as the eldest, now that she had an older brother.

By coincidence, I was scheduled to attend a museum security conference in Washington in February 1995. It would not take much to pay my own way to London from there, to meet them all and catch up with my son, Nick, who had moved to the UK a few years earlier. Gill and David were excited at the prospect.

On the way over to London, I visited my cousin Mary in Philadelphia. She was the daughter of Bill who had travelled to America after the First World War. Bill and his wife, another Mary, had both died. My cousin, of all the family, knew most about our history. She was also interested in the search I was undertaking. It was her dad Bill who had fathered a child, married the mother and left for America, leaving them both behind. Cousin Mary had a half-brother born in East Ham who was now dead. With both her parents and the boy's mother also dead, my cousin was never going to unravel that family secret. It was good, particularly at that time, to be reminded of Mum's side of the family, scattered as they were throughout the world. Not since those Christmases at Barrington Road had I been together with so many of the Farrell whānau as gathered around me in Philadelphia for those few days I was there. Snow was still piled up on the pavements when I left New York for London. I thought of Mum and how travelling to Liverpool had been such a journey for her.

My son Nick married Anna, whom he had met while working as a journalist. I spent some days with them in High Wycombe before going to London for the meeting with my father's family. Nick and Anna had just mortgaged themselves to capacity to get into the house they were living in. It was comfortable in the way a student flat could be comfortable. Nick was very supportive of what I was doing, interested in his new uncles, aunts and cousins, but did not feel it involved him. He said I had always been open to him about my parentage so had guessed that sooner or later I would do something about finding my father. He and Anna seemed happy together. Having made the same journey I made in 1965, but in reverse, Nick encountered difficulties similar to mine in settling into a new country. His coping and avoidance mechanisms had also been similar to mine, and now here he was in a new marriage and in a new house, perhaps wondering what life held in store for him. Back in New Zealand, his sister Kay had chosen a completely different and perhaps more settled path. They couldn't be more different, but we had been through a lot together and I loved them both. I needed to keep that in mind as I spent my last night without siblings.

The phone box stank of stale urine. My breath smoked against the glass in the cold morning air as I stamped amongst the fag ends to keep my feet warm. Shivering, I slotted in the phone card and dialled the familiar number. It was ringing, my umbilical cord to the summer world where I belonged. I gripped the receiver tightly. It was sticky with the stale cold sweat of others.

"How's it going?" There were no preliminaries. Sue had been expecting the call. She sounded slightly breathless.

"I'm at High Wycombe station, waiting to get the train to London. It's started." I felt a desperate sense of loneliness. Sue said the previous three months had been like living with someone who was having an intense love affair, what with the strange handwriting on letters and those long whispered phone calls in the middle of the night.

The line to New Zealand crackled and I had to bend into the corner of the booth to catch her reply through the static.

"I wish I was there with you, but this is something you're going to have to do by yourself. Just remember, whatever happens, I'll be here for you." I could picture her on the stool by the phone. The setting sun would be flooding into the sitting room of our house, perched on the Wellington hills.

"It's still bloody dark, yet its 8.00am. I'd forgotten what winter does to everybody here." I looked out at the commuters struggling miserably for their particular spot on the platform. Nothing much had changed. I had been part of all that once. "It's difficult to describe how I'm feeling right now, but it's one of those times when all I can do is withdraw and watch myself performing upon some remote stage. It's very weird."

Sue had lived with me long enough to understand my way of coping with pressure.

"When do you meet them?" she asked. "I want to be sure I'm awake for that."

"I'm meeting them at Marylebone at midday." I looked at my watch. "Another four hours."

"If one thing's certain," she laughed, "it's that you'll be early for them! I do love you."

"Just remember it's taken me nearly sixty years to get to this. And I wouldn't be here at this moment if it wasn't for the certain knowledge you'd be around to catch me if it all turns to shit." I could see the commuters readying themselves to fight for seats on the next London train. They were like clockwork toys, bumping and crashing into one another, eyes firmly fixed on the middle distance.

"It's time I was on my way," I said. "I just want to get on with it now. I'll ring you when I can."

The southern hemisphere sun dipped behind a cloud as I gently slotted the receiver back onto the cradle. I pushed the phone box door and it squeaked in protest as it opened to allow me to move onto the crowded platform.

The doors of the train hissed open, and I was carried inside on a tide of bodies. I found myself pushed into a window seat, my legs threaded between those of the woman opposite. We avoided eye contact. The man next to me opened his newspaper in a gesture of disengagement and dismissal. I knew the unwritten laws of London travel. I had been there before.

My identikit reflection in the carriage window looked back at me as we swayed though the outer suburbs of the city. My father's eyes returned my stare. I had inherited his stoop, his thinning hair and the quizzical lazy eyebrows, but the doggedness in the tilt of the chin came from Mum. I was startled at how Jewish I was looking these days.

Had that journey started the previous year, it could have been my father who was coming to meet me. Instead, it was his daughter and other son who were going to be at Marylebone Station.

As the train drew into the terminus at Marylebone, my reflection disappeared into the flickering grey dawn. I shrank back into my seat as others busied themselves in the leaving ritual they performed every workday. I was in no hurry. I had another pang of anxiety as I moved down the empty carriage towards the door and onto the platform. I hoped Mum would understand what I was about to do and would forgive me.

Normally I would be happy to spend three hours killing time in London, but that day there was too much to think about. I walked familiar London streets and ended up at the National Gallery, hoping the sight of the Van Goghs would calm me. I decided to buy something to read while I waited at Marylebone Station. What would they expect or hope their brother to be reading? *Plays and Player,* perhaps, for David, the actor, or *Times Educational Supplement* for Gill, the social worker? My preference, with anxiety rapidly disassembling my mind like mud on a shaking fault line, was more inclined to a football fan magazine. I took down the *New Statesman.* I knew that Left would be much safer political territory than Right, although continual exposure to New Zealand politics and politicians had driven me into a cynical, neutral corner. I thought Mum and Shaw would be a little disappointed with that, but it was becoming increasingly difficult to differentiate Left from Right and Good from Bad. Those things had been simpler in the immediate post-war years.

It was 11.45am. Time for yet another pee and a final personal appearance check. It would hardly do for them to discover their brand new brother from New Zealand lounging about at Marylebone Station with his flies undone. I selected a bench with a clear view of the underground exit for the Northern Line and settled back, studiously opening the *New Statesman,* gazing without comprehension at the jumbled words before me.

Another check of the time. The curse of someone unhealthily early for everything. 11.55am.

Suppose they were late? Suppose I'd got the station venue wrong? Suppose they'd changed their minds? The letters and phone calls had been very reassuring and welcoming, but Morris's secret had been tightly held for nearly sixty years. Who knew what second thoughts his other children might be having?

There was some movement at the top of the escalator. They had seen me first and were waving, although we were only a few yards from one another. I stood watching them as they came towards me. Rehearsed words were left unsaid as we simply held one another with the clumsiness of strangers, giggling in disbelief at the enormity of what we were doing. I resisted the urge to touch their faces, to trace the genetic imprints of our father. At that moment I needed to feel their physical presence and was comforted as we whispered stilted endearments, like lovers. We pulled apart, slightly embarrassed, regarding one another carefully.

The examination continued in the taxi on the way to lunch at a nearby restaurant. As I talked to one of them, I was aware of the other's eyes upon me.

"God, I can't believe how like him you are." David smiled as I returned his unabashed stare. He was taller, but otherwise it was like looking in the mirror.

"When I saw you at the station just now, it could have been him sitting there. Except for the beard." He said, indicating my short-cropped, greying beard which, in vanity, I had nurtured to compensate the indignity of thinning hair, which I saw then was our father's gift to both his sons.

Gill's letters and phone calls to me in New Zealand had been warm, but I sensed that she was more aware than David of the risks this new brother could pose to the family and to her father's reputation. Her caution was understandable. A shared parent does not ensure shared affection or values. Pity I'd left the *New Statesman* on the bench at

Marylebone in the excitement of the meeting. The sight of that would have reassured her I was not a John Major Tory.

It was to be a champagne lunch at a discreetly expensive restaurant. The elaborately folded deep red table napkins contrasted tastefully with crisp white tablecloths. Silver cutlery nestled against delicate champagne flutes. The service was, for me, uncomfortably deferential, but we were left alone as the alcohol worked to ease the tension.

"What I can't understand about all this is why you left it so long. Six months ago, you knew nothing about us and we didn't even know of your existence," David said. We were done with the preliminaries. I expected this question, but not quite so soon. David had a way of moving his hands, palms up, which I had noticed on the *Miss Marple* video. In this context, it seemed almost Jewish.

"That's a question I've often asked myself." I hesitated. It was time Morris was brought to the table. "It's probably a combination of a lot of things, but in the end, it came down to not wanting to expose myself to further rejection from our father. It was only in the last year I felt sufficiently secure in myself and my relationships at home to risk rejection." David blinked and looked away briefly. I later found that we were both easily brought to tears.

"Now Mary doesn't have to keep Morris's secret, she seems almost relieved we know," Gill said. "She's looking forward to meeting you, although she has told her neighbours you are a cousin from New Zealand." Gill seemed to be seeking reassurance about her mother. I didn't think Mary had anything to apologise for. There was something dignified about her wanting to protect her husband's reputation. She had certainly opened out in her letters to me. I had rung her a few days earlier when I had arrived at Heathrow. She had said then, "You are enhancing our lives."

Morris continued to dominate our conversation. I realised they were still adjusting to the stark fact of our father's behaviour all those years ago. They seemed to be reconciling that with what they knew of him as an exemplary parent, grandparent, scholar and, ironically, a leader in the field of institutional child welfare. For me, he was beginning to take a human form, which I would have to put alongside the myth I had created about him. First a war hero, then a pariah and now, possibly, just a man who made a mistake. I was still not ready to reconcile myself to that last person, although he was emerging as bright, egotistical, argumentative, great fun and totally devoted to his immediate family. I had convinced myself one of the reasons he left Mum was because Mary offered a safe passage to the gentile middle class. I had suckled the vinegar of the English class system at my mother's breast, and her prejudices were mine.

We continued to examine one another like exhibits at a waxworks. I watched Gill as she fiddled absently with her cutlery. It was the structure of her hands that carried Morris's imprint. We would have a perfect match if we placed palms together. She caught me looking and smiled, shaking her head in bemusement.

"It hardly seems he's dead," she said. "Mum has said that they knew you had gone to New Zealand after *your* mum died, but she didn't say how they knew that."

"I'm sure Morris and Mum were at Red Hill School together, just before and at the start of the war. The principal there was a man called Otto Shaw." I noticed a flicker of recognition from Gill. She knew the name. "Red Hill was an innovative, experimental environment that took difficult kids who mainstream institutions couldn't cope with."

"Mum continued working for him after I was born, until she died, in fact. It was just after her funeral that Shaw told me that he had been speaking with my father." I told them about the words Shaw had used: *you won't be hearing anything from that source.*

"Dad often talked about Shaw as if he was a mentor," Gill said. "I never met the man, but I certainly have heard about him and the regime he ran at Red Hill. I knew our mother resented the relationship. I used to think it was jealousy." Gill sipped reflectively on her champagne. "Do you think Shaw played any part in all this?"

"I'm certain he acted as a go-between for Mum and Morris after

Morris left Red Hill. His words after Mum's funeral left me in no doubt that he was still in touch with Morris. Shaw could be very manipulative and had an intimidating presence about him." I sipped some water, aware how much I was talking. "On the other hand, he was capable of great acts of kindness and I have benefited a lot from his interventions on my behalf. There is no question that Red Hill under him was very successful in turning around the lives of many of the kids who went through that system." We were already onto dessert – Gill and David called it 'pudding'. "Shaw was a great fan of A.S.Neill. Schools like Summerhill and Red Hill needed charismatic people like them as leaders if they were to work. Mum held Shaw in awe, although I know from some of the letters she left behind and what I saw myself that she wasn't afraid to take him on. Yeah, I think you could be right, Gill. It's a pity Shaw is dead too. We all might have a few questions for him."

"I think it's going to be okay. The conversations are like minefields but, so far, there have been no major explosions." I was on the phone to Sue from Gill's house. I felt like a reporter filing a story from the other side of the world.

"What are they like?" Sue asked, "It must have been hard for them, with their father dying so recently."

"They've been incredibly generous in their responses, given the shock and grief they must be feeling. I'm a bit ashamed that I never considered how all this has been for them." Sue was right, of course. I had given no thought at all to how my appearance may have affected them so soon after their father had died. I had fifty or so years to prepare for that meeting. For them, it had only been a matter of weeks.

"I like them both and I think they like me. We've laughed and we've cried together. So that's a start. We've also speculated what Morris and Mum would have made of today. We came to the conclusion that they would've been glad it had happened but would've been very happy not to have been here." I hesitated. "I still feel that somehow I am being disloyal to Mum."

Late that evening, I met Gemma, Gill's daughter, at Gill's house.

She seemed delighted to meet her new uncle. She called me *the skeleton in grandpa's cupboard,* but she was devoted to her grandpa and clearly missed him being around. Nathan, Gemma's elder brother also had fond memories of his grandpa but was welcoming and not particularly fazed by the entry of a new uncle. John, Gill's husband, was also there. He had described himself as a Geordie with a capital 'G'. I had not considered how people not directly involved with my search might be affected. If John had any concerns about having a new brother-in-law, he hid it and was a warm and hospitable host. David returned with his eldest son, Tom, and we all crowded into Gill's sitting room. Tom was accepting of the situation and of me but was still grieving for the grandpa who had played such an important part in his life. Tom's younger brother, Francis, turned up later. He was a quietly personable young man. Tall, with long flowing black hair, it was less easy to see the physical likeness that was there with the other cousins, but he was just as welcoming.

Gill and I relaxed in one another's company. We enjoyed the next day wrapped up against the cold wandering around Crouch End, a part of North London I did not know. There was of course endless speculation about Morris's relationship with my Mum and with Mary. There were reputations to protect for all the parties involved and we accepted we would never really know what happened. We were in a bookshop in Crouch End when we bumped into someone that Gill knew.

"This is my brother Peter from New Zealand," Gill said brightly, much to my great pleasure.

"I didn't know you had a brother out there, Gill," he said shaking my hand.

"Ah, well," Gill stuttered. Having said the words, she was not quite ready for the obvious follow-up question. "That's a long story," she ended up enigmatically. We left the shop giggling.

"I suppose I should have said '*I didn't know I had a brother either'!*" she laughed.

We worked out we must have been together in the same part of London and attended some of the same dance halls in the early sixties.

That started a further run of speculation – supposing she had turned up at home with this Peter she had met at a dance? How would Morris have reacted to that? It started us off giggling again. I was beginning to enjoy having a sister.

David's terraced house in Stoke Newington was narrow and tall, with four storeys. It was full of books but there was no obvious sign of theatrical memorabilia. He was pleased he had just landed a part at the National Theatre, which fitted in very well with TV shootings of episodes of *The Bill* and *Just William.* This was heady stuff for me to take in, but it was just work for him. He had always been an actor. I wondered how he managed the insecurities of his profession, maintaining his talent at the highest level and coping with the pressures of two young adults at home.

Like Gill, David was genuinely interested to learn about where I was from, and so we went down to East Ham and stood outside 32 Barrington Road. Together we looked up at the attic bedroom where I had been born. The house looked much the same as I recalled, but there was some bleakness about the area that I didn't remember from the last time I was there. As a seven year old, when I was up from Red Hill, I used to wait under the railway arches for Uncle George to come home from his job at the printers. With the odd needle and condom lying around, the arches were obviously being used for a totally different purpose these days.

Back in Stoke Newington, we went to a supermarket. David had already explained that he had followed Morris's lead as far as the Jewish faith was concerned, so we did not need to dwell at the kosher food counter. He said that their (our) cousins, Uncle Bernard's children, were practising Jews but they did not see much of them. Aunt Rose was still alive, but Mary had asked that she not be told about me.

As we talked about ourselves and tried to recover some of those lost fifty or so years, we discovered some very similar characteristics. We were both obsessive about sport; David with cricket and me with football. Neither of us had achieved much academically at school, but we both seemed to have turned things around a bit after that. My stage work at school and with the Sutton Valence Women's Institute was insignificant alongside his, but there was a shared interest there. Most of all, we found we laughed at the ridiculousness of life in general and ourselves in particular. Sometimes David would have to stop the car whilst we recovered from hysterical fits of laughter at some observation that only we would find funny.

The death of Morris was still raw for him and he would suddenly find himself brought to tears when describing some aspect of our father's character. We watched a video of a TV play David had been in, called *Finding Sarah*. David had been quite pleased with the way his role turned out. Apparently Morris often referred to it and was insistent that it was one of the better plays David had been in. It was about a woman looking for her birth mother. David played the part of the disgruntled husband.

"I used to wonder why he was such a fan of that," David said. "But I think I know now why he liked it."

David and Gill did all they could to connect with my past. David and I went together to Sussex to meet Phyllis, and Gill trailed round Kent with me to see what was left of Red Hill, including visiting Mum's grave at East Sutton Church. The hop field behind the graveyard had been pulled out and replaced by a golf course. Later, Gill's husband John did some research about Morris's background and we went into Whitechapel to stand in the street where he was born and outside the school he attended. The old map, drawn up in 1900, indicated the area was the Jewish Quarter of London.

Mary Horovitch was waiting for the three of us in the hall of the large house at Shenfield. She was a tiny brittle woman. We hugged briefly, and she whispered to me, "What took you so long?" She didn't want an answer, and I couldn't give her one. There was a vagueness about her that I thought hid an inner toughness and a very sharp mind. She had already been quite forthcoming in her letters, and I knew not to rush things. I was very aware that my father had been living in that house just six months previously, used the toilet, brushed his teeth, wrote his thesis. Everything. His presence was everywhere. David caught me running my fingers over the chair in the study, feeling for the indentations in the leather. In the bathroom I held Morris's old hairbrush, touching the grey hair lodged in the bristles. The three of us held one another again and wept for our own separate reasons. Mary looked on and smiled her vague secret smile. She did seem pleased to see us together.

Later I went back to Shenfield on my own as Mary wanted to talk, just her and me. She was a little deaf so I sat close to her as she poured the tea. I did not want to sit in the larger chair opposite. That had obviously been Morris's chair. I had seen a photo of him in it. We talked generalities about New Zealand, politics and what had happened to me since I emigrated. I explained that, although she and I were not related at all, Māori would regard us as extended family or 'whānau'.

I was not sure she was listening to me. Perhaps it was the deafness or perhaps she was waiting for me to introduce Morris into the conversation. I would need to be patient for her to trust me with any real insights.

"I think my mother met Morris when they were working for a Major Faithfull at Hazeleigh Court in the 1930s," I said, as a way of moving the conversation on a bit.

She smiled her distant smile as she searched for the words to reply. "I was at Hazeleigh too you know. I used to go down there at weekends to help out." She seemed almost relieved at the turn the conversation had taken. "Morris and I became great friends. He was a good talker. Knew about lots of things and liked to show off his knowledge. It was an intellectual thing between us then. He was fascinated with the writings of Bernard Shaw and the Fabian socialists."

"Did you meet my mother there?" I questioned gently.

"Oh, yes. Marion was a great worker. She used to turn out wonderful meals." I felt myself bridle on Mum's behalf, but I was beginning to get used to Mary's frank and sometimes insensitive observations, which seemed to be delivered without malice. "I always felt she never had the chance to reach her potential either at Hazeleigh or later at Red Hill."

"Major Faithfull was a vet, wasn't he? Bit of an eccentric by all accounts." I had done some research on Faithfull and Hazeleigh.

"Seems like Hazeleigh was a bit unusual for the times."

"That's why I liked going down there. It was a very unusual and exciting place for someone like me." She looked at me directly then continued, "I didn't like Faithfull much. He had very loose morals. It was common knowledge he was always having affairs with the women on his staff." I did not quite know what to make of that, but it became clearer when she added, "*I* never did, of course, but I think Marion may have."

I was long past the age when I was embarrassed by Mum's sexual past. I guessed that she must have been active in that respect, if only from the company she kept, so I was not particularly surprised at what Mary was telling me.

I waited for her to break the brief silence between us.

"I was not ready to get engaged or anything, and so Morris and I drifted apart. We didn't get together again until he left Red Hill." She hesitated briefly. "He told me all about his affair with Marion. He said she thought she was too old to conceive. He and Marion had been friends, but he always said he had never loved anyone else but me."

Maybe she was telling me the truth, but I hoped that she was embroidering things a little.

She had a way of completely avoiding any questions she did not want to answer and I knew there was no point pursuing this further. She told me about the Quaker wedding she and Morris had in Haslemere. Both families apparently had reservations about the match. "But we were pretty determined and they all came round in the end," she said.

She described the last time she had seen me at Red Hill, when she and Morris had visited. It must have been about 1942, before Gill was born she thought. "It was a rather difficult visit I remember. Everyone, including Shaw, ignored me. Marion was the only one who welcomed me." She smiled gently, "I remember she brought us a cup of tea in bed." It was a scenario that raised a lot of questions, but I sensed I was never going to know the purpose of the visit. I secretly applauded what I thought might have been Mum's gesture of defiance.

Having unburdened herself and said what she wanted to say, Mary was happy to just talk about Morris and their family. I learned more about his Jewish childhood and how he abandoned the faith. He had been intolerant of his own parents' and his brother's unswerving commitment to Judaism. He had stayed in specialist teaching roles after leaving Red Hill and ended up as superintendent/principal at Hutton Poplars Residential Home, a large specialist institution with about 350 residents. After his retirement he became active in the Labour Party and lectured in residential childcare at the West London Institute. At eighty-two he was awarded a Master of Arts degree in politics and government. Gill had already sent me the newspaper clippings of that event. Mary described a warm caring husband and father to their children. She thought he had been a wonderful grandfather. By the time she had finished, the late winter sun had dipped behind the trees and there was a chill in the darkening room. She did not move to turn on the lights.

In the face of all I was hearing of Morris's virtue, intellect and knowledge of children, the obvious question remained unanswered: why did my father not contact his eldest son? I tried to think of something I could ask that perhaps addressed that yawning gap in my knowledge.

"He sounds an incredible man, Mary, but I can't help wondering if he thought about me at all." It was my turn to look directly at her. "Did he ever talk to you about me after you got married? Did he remain in touch with Shaw at Red Hill?" I was asking too many questions, but I could not help myself. She was quiet, thinking about what she was going to say.

"I don't want you to get the wrong impression about him." I could barely hear her. "He loved to talk and be at the centre of things. He was a bit of a show-off really and could be overbearing. In the years before he died he became quite short-tempered." She hesitated. Her sentences tumbled out in no particular order, but she was trying to get to answer the question that was so important to me. "He had lots of women friends and liked to hold court, but he was always faithful," she said firmly. "He was a warm man who loved to cuddle." She had already told me that when she had written those letters a few months previously. I had to be careful not to take too much from what she was saying and why she was saying it.

"As for Shaw," she continued, "I never liked him and the influence he seemed to have over Morris. They were both involved in the Association of Workers for Maladjusted Children, and they met at those meetings. But they also met at other times over the years." Mary said she never went to those meetings, but she knew Morris would receive information about my progress in New Zealand. Apparently the last time they met was in 1976, shortly before Shaw died. According to Mary, Shaw flew his own plane up to Southend and met Morris there.

"Shaw died soon after that, and we didn't hear any more about you." She looked into the middle distance, gathering her thoughts "Once, when he was coming to the end of his degree course, he said he was going to Red Hill to get some background. I guessed the real reason for the visit was to find out something about you."

"That was quite a trip for him. He must have been eighty," I said. He didn't have a driver's licence, so that would have meant a journey by different trains through London to Maidstone and then a bus to Red Hill from Maidstone. A round trip of possibly six hours.

"Yes, it was but he was determined to do it. When he came back he said he had heard that you were still in New Zealand and doing well." She smiled, satisfied she had given me a small gift. "He was very happy. I knew all along that was all he went to Red Hill for." I wondered who Morris had spoken to at Red Hill. Phyllis was the holder of all the secrets, but she had already told me all she knew and made no mention of a visit.

"Thanks, Mary." We were in the hall, and I was slipping on my coat and scarf before going out into the cold. "You have been amazing the way you have managed all this so soon after he died."

We hugged briefly, and she smiled that smile of hers. "You're not like him at all, you know. You look like him, but you're not like him. You're... much better tempered."

Mum would not have appreciated being part of Mary's whānau, but she may have allowed herself a bitter, ironic smile at Mary's implied complaint about Morris.

Time was running out before I had to be back in New Zealand, and we all needed a break from the emotional maelstrom in which we had found ourselves. I went to stay with my friend Angela, whom I had known from my days at the Kent County Library. We had seen one another through a few relationship crises over the years, but she now seemed settled with her new partner. It was she who reminded me of the times I turned up at her council house in Chatham when we first met. It is unsurprising that I was drawn to her family. Angela was the eldest of three children who all seemed to get on so well with one another. Her dad was a quietly spoken, smiley man who loved to paint. Her mum held everything together and was the cornerstone of the family. I always felt welcome in that house. Angela believed I idealised her family although the reality was somewhat different from what I saw. That may have been so, but both Angela and Grace, her mother, became mainstays in my life for as long as they lived.

The only member of my own immediate family from the Barrington Road days still left in London was my cousin Jo. It was Jo who had been present at my birth. She was still living in the house in Ilford where she had been born. Her parents had both died. The attractive vital young girl I remembered had grown into a reclusive, eccentric old woman. Her consuming passion was the local theatre group in Ilford. She was still a talented amateur actor, wigmaker and costume designer. Visiting her was like visiting Miss Havisham. All that was lacking were the cobwebs. Most things were in the same place they had been in the 1940s except for a television set and what looked like a rest home for retired wigs. Keeping contact with her from New Zealand had been difficult as she never wrote letters, but I could see she was very interested in my story. I thought she might have some insights as she would have been old enough to listen in to the adults' conversations in the way children do. Jo had always admired Marion above all her aunts, as Marion was fun and had an air of mystery about her.

Jo told me to rummage through a desk drawer to see if I could find any photos of interest. While I was looking through the faded brown photos, she tried to recollect fifty year old conversations.

"I remember one Christmas, when you were about five, you got a bike or a wheelbarrow or something like that." It was a bike and it had soot on the wheels, but I didn't want to interrupt her. "Marion said Father Christmas had been very good to Peter that year. There was a slight edge to her voice. Ironic, I suppose you'd call it." Jo hesitated. "Do you think it came from your father?"

"I don't know, Jo. It's a possibility. Mum didn't have much money," I said.

"There was another time when you had been here with Marion. My mum and a couple of the others were talking after you had gone." She screwed up her face, memorising the words. "One of them said Peter was very lucky to have a second family and something about Jews being very good with families."

"Looks like my Mum must have told them a bit more than I thought," I said. For a family that usually operated on nods, winks and body language, this was quite a revealing conversation Jo had overheard.

Jo left to go into the kitchen and I carried on sorting through the photos to see if there was anything of interest. At the back of the drawer was a bundle of letters in a large manila envelope. I pulled them out excitedly. So much had unfolded in the last week or two – could this be another revelation? I was disappointed and touched at the same time as I recognised the New Zealand stamps and my own wriggly handwriting. Jo had kept all my letters from the first one I had sent from National Park. I flicked through a few of the earlier ones. They were full of innocent optimism and enthusiasm for my new surroundings with descriptions of sunshine and beaches which I hardly saw in that first year. I smiled to myself as I slipped them back in the envelope. They were, I supposed, harmless lies.

On the train back to London I reflected upon my visit. Jo's

mother had been very possessive, particularly after Uncle Steve died. Any potential Jo may have had was smothered out of her from a very early age. I compared this to the way Mum allowed me freedom and independence at Red Hill. Some of this would have been driven by necessity, caused by the demands of her job, but mostly it was a deliberate choice. I was beginning to understand the sacrifices she had made for me.

I told Gill and David about Jo's account of conversations she had overheard. They thought the Christmas bike may have come from Morris. I was not confident that was the case, but by then, we were worn out trying to find explanations for the unexplainable. We had one final get-together at Gill's house, and I noticed how well Gill and David's children related to one another. It was as if they were brothers and sisters rather than cousins.

My love for David and Gill startled me. It was totally unexpected and all the more so because it seemed to be reciprocated. I could hardly feel anger towards my father, given the generosity of spirit and the love shown to me by his wife, children and grandchildren.

I had left New Zealand to find more about the father I never knew. Like a forensic character examination, I found traces of myself there. My father and I evidently shared good humour, compassion, warmth and sensitivity, as well as less desirable traits such as stubbornness, a tendency towards hypocrisy and some arrogance. Morris may have seen himself as a working class intellectual, and he seemed to have enjoyed being the centre of attention. Neither characteristic is shared by his eldest son. I found a man I think I could have liked, and I think he could have liked me.

The search for some clues about his relationship with Mum was incomplete and would probably remain so. Perhaps she hoped the poetry she left behind for me to see would be explanation enough. Perhaps she regretted the missed opportunity to tell me more when I was seventeen and first learned my father was still alive. Sadly, I did not have the maturity to ask the questions of her that would have helped unpick the fiction that surrounded that part of her life.

What I am left with is the knowledge that the lie constructed all those years ago has, in the end, proved to be harmless. My life has been richer for the upbringing she gave me and the sacrifices she made. That is all that matters.

Sue and me in the Cook Islands, 1994. It was on this holiday that I decided the time was right to look for my father.

Talking to the New Zealand Jewish community on the marae at Te Papa, 1998.

AFTERWORD

SOME LOOSE ENDS

Of the institutions where Mum spent over half her life, Colney Hatch is closed and has been converted to luxury apartments called Princes Park Manor. Red Hill School is also closed and has been substantially refurbished; as Charlton Court Place, the buildings and grounds have been converted to a tasteful, very expensive gated housing development, complete with security systems.

Waikune Prison was closed in 1986. The shell of the building remains like some decaying carcass at the side of the main state highway. All the staff houses, including the one Brenda and I lived in for two years, have been moved off the site.

Morris's wife Mary died in 2002. She was ninety-two. Her final act of generosity was remembering me in her will. I owe her so much, but I think the emergence of the skeleton from Morris's cupboard also added something to the final years of her life.

I have returned frequently to the UK since I first found this new family, sometimes with Sue, sometimes on my own. Always I have spent time with Gill and David.

After Mary died, the embargo on meeting the Jewish side of the family was lifted. Morris's brother Bernard seems to have been a mild man, perhaps a bit overwhelmed by his elder brother. Morris was known to be impatient with him, possibly because of Bernard's firm adherence to the Jewish faith. Bernard had changed his surname by deed poll. People with Jewish-sounding names were known to change their name during the war, particularly if they went into the armed forces. In 2003 Aunt Rose, Bernard's widow, was told about me just before Sue and I arrived in the UK on a visit. A meeting was arranged at a kosher restaurant in Stanmore, Middlesex. Aunt Rose had three sons, two were married. They were all waiting in line on the pavement outside the restaurant to greet us when we arrived. I was getting used to that type of meeting and was relatively calm. Sue grabbed my hand. This was the first time she had been involved in anything quite like that. She was excited and nervous but relishing the drama of it all. We moved through the line like royalty at a command performance, although I was aware they were examining me as closely as I was examining them. I saw some of myself reflected in the Horovitch features, and they could see a lot of their uncle in their new cousin.

Over the meal there was an interesting exchange between one of the sons and Aunt Rose.

"Do you think Dad knew anything about Peter, Mum?" he asked his mother.

Rose shook her head. "No," she said emphatically, with her palms up. "If Bernard had known, then *I* would have known."

I was to sit next to Aunt Rose at that dinner. She was very interested in the exact dates of Morris's relationship with Mum. She seemed to be matching those up with what she thought was going on with her brother-in-law Morris at the time. She kept looking at me intently. "You do look like him, you know. Sometimes, it's just like having him sitting here."

Sue and I went back to Red Hill School in 2003. The school had kept going for some years after Shaw died but finally closed in 1992. When we visited, the buildings and outbuildings were in the process of being converted to Charlton Court Place. I was surprised that Allan Rimmer, the principal who succeeded Shaw, still had an office in the complex. I had vaguely known of him before I left for New Zealand, mainly because he was on a small list of colleagues whose name Mum could only repeat if she preceded it by a mild expletive of some sort. I didn't know why it was 'bloody' Allan Rimmer, but it was evident to me that she did not like him much. When we met him, he seemed slightly evasive. He said he did not know about Morris and had never met him.

"What was Marion like?" Sue asked in her direct way.

"I would describe her as an angry person. She was a bit rough and ready." His perspective was not a surprise.

It was odd he should deny knowing Morris, because I found a letter to him from Morris dated 20 June 1988. Morris's spidery handwriting had not changed from the time he wrote to Mum all those years previously about the financial arrangements he had put in place following my birth.

I knew from Mary that Morris made a visit to Red Hill about this time:

Dear Allan

Thank-you very much for making my visit to Red Hill not only possible but such a delight. I am not usually given to nostalgia. My golden age is with the present and the past was not all that easy a time for me. I enjoyed my experience of Red Hill and Shaw and Holland and Sleight and Marion Farrell but it was also a great testing time and I did not always score an upper-second. To be frank, I appreciated the work of Otto Shaw (Shaw he was then, Otto he was later) and was confident of his success. But I was never really quite at home at Red Hill (or anywhere else) at the time so my visit was in no sense a homecoming. But I have no wish now to develop those thoughts. I must repeat that the day was very enjoyable and it would take too long to explain why.

There is no direct mention of me in the letter, and it is likely Rimmer did not know Morris was my father until I told him. I tried a number of times to get more information from Rimmer through email after I got back to New Zealand, but he did not respond. He has since died.

On that same visit I arranged for additional lettering to be chipped out on Mum's gravestone at East Sutton Church. The new lettering says simply "Arohanui" – much love. I was pleased to hear later that some ex-Red Hill boys visited MOF's grave following a reunion, noticed the new lettering and recognised the New Zealand connection.

Through my daughter Kay and with Sue's help, I have learned to be a granddad to my three grandchildren. I also have another grandchild who lives in Malaysia with his mother. I am determined they should all know they have a granddad who loves them. Nick and Anna separated; Nick now lives in Rome with Paola.

Gill and John have been out to New Zealand twice, and David has been here once. It does sometimes feel as though I have been brought up with them both. I have seen David perform on stage. He is obviously an accomplished actor. I feel a real sense of pride watching him perform. Once, we saw him at Guildford where he was in a revival of a J.B.

Priestley play which later went on to the West End. At the interval, two bejewelled women were talking about the play. One of them said "I think David Horovitch is just brilliant. I have seen him in so many things now. And I often hear him on radio."

Sue nudged me. "That's your brother they are talking about," she whispered.

After Te Papa opened and just before I left, there was a celebration for the Jewish people of New Zealand on the new marae at the museum. I had by then found my extended family, my whānau. One of the kuia (female leader) who was among those who had encouraged me to start my search said I should attend the celebration and speak on the marae.

"Why would I do that?" I said. "I am not Jewish." Yet I knew I would have to go. She would arrange it.

So it was in 1998 that I stood nervously on the marae at Te Papa, cleared my throat and said:

"You may wonder what a cockney man born in 1940 with Yiddish-speaking Jewish grandparents and a father he did not know is doing addressing an assembly of Jewish people on this beautiful marae in New Zealand. Welcome to our marae. I am Peter Farrell, and I would like to tell you a little of my story and what whānau means to me..."

END

SOURCES AND FURTHER READING

This is a memoir. Most of the material derives from the author's own memory, interviews/discussions with participants or from documents, notes and family records he holds. In some cases, particularly in the prison sequences, some names have been changed.

Other sources are:

BOOKS

Croall, Jonathon, *Neill of Summerhill: The Permanent Rebel* (London, Routledge & K. Paul, 1983)

Dakers, Caroline, *The Countryside at War, 1914-1918* (London, Constable, 1987)

Faithfull, Marianne with Dalton, David, *Faithfull* (London, Michael Joseph, 1994)

Hunter, Richard and Macalpine, Ida, *Psychiatry for the Poor ... a medical and social history*, Dawsons, 1974). Includes Colney Hatch Asylum.

Shaw, Otto L., *Maladjusted Boys* (London, Allen & Unwin, 1965)

Shaw, Otto L., *Prisons of the Mind* (London, Allen & Unwin, 1969)

ARCHIVES ETC.

I am grateful for the assistance from:

Archives New Zealand, Wellington: Papers concerning author's immigration to New Zealand.

London Metropolitan Archives: Papers concerning Marion Farrell at Colney Hatch Mental Institution 1928.

Planned Environment Therapy Trust Archive, Toddington, Cheltenham: Papers concerning Otto L. Shaw and Red Hill School, including comprehensive accounts by Ralph Gee and other ex-pupils of Red Hill School. This archive also holds personal papers of Marion Farrell and an oral history the author recorded with the archive's Senior Archivist, Dr Craig Fees, in 2010.

Red Hill School: Official website: http://redhill.kkb.in.th/

University of Strathclyde, Glasgow: Papers concerning Major Theodore J. Faithfull, the Woodcraft Folk and Priory Gate School.

I have tried to make contact with all individuals and copyright owners for their permission to reproduce material. I apologise for any unintentional errors or omissions and would, of course, like to hear about any corrections so these could be included in future printings.

AUTHOR'S NOTE

Among other things, this book is a testament to the path of reconciliation and understanding that my half-brother and sister followed with me over the many years since we first met in 1995. I remain incredibly grateful to them for their generosity in accepting me and sharing with me our respective family histories and experiences.

Since the publication of the first edition of the book, irreconcilable differences of opinion have surfaced concerning my interpretation of some aspects of those histories, particularly surrounding our father and their mother. Perhaps such differences within the whānau were inevitable given the circumstances which brought about that first meeting.

This book remains my personal history, seen through my eyes and/or informed by my research and understanding of events and people.

ACKNOWLEDGEMENTS

So many people have lived this memoir with me over the years. You will know who you are. Some of you will have participated in the action and some as cheerleaders when the going got tough. To all of you, thank you.

The writing part all started with Dame Fiona Kidman who has remained a mentor, as has Norman Bilbrough. I have talented friends who have, over many years, helped with feedback, encouragement and preliminary editorial pedantry, which only good friends can share with one another. In that connection I particularly mention Ruth Allan, Alan Rooney, Pete and Raewyn Pointon, Lyn Adams, Jan Pryor and Rae Nicholl.

I am sad that Angela Abell, a friend from Kent County Library days, and Linda Raffell in England did not live to see the completion of the work to which they contributed so much.

John Plumb in England and Gren Bell in New Zealand, both prison inspectors in their respective countries, checked the authenticity of the material about prisons.

Professor John Spiers has provided invaluable help and advice on the whole project. Dr Len Bloom and Ralph Gee provided assistance with the Red Hill School material.

Linda Niccol, Chris Mahoney and Rebecca Horrocks from Mission Hall have been instrumental in getting this book from words on a page to a printed book I am proud of. Jenny Argante from Oceanbooks, also a friend from Kent County Library days, Susan Tarr and Penny Griffith each contributed in their own way to the final product.

The book is all about whānau, and I am particularly fortunate with mine in the UK, New Zealand, Italy, United Arab Emirates, Australia, USA and Malaysia.

Finally, it all comes down to one person. Sue Christie has always been there and remains an inspiration without whom there would have been no happy ending.

ABOUT THE AUTHOR

Peter Farrell was born in London in 1940 and immigrated to New Zealand in 1965.

He has had a varied career in the public sector, mostly in change management roles. He was a director at the National Museum and Art Gallery when it moved to the Wellington waterfront and reopened as Te Papa in 1998.

He studied creative writing with Fiona Kidman before gaining an advanced diploma in applied arts (creative writing) from Whitireia Community Polytechnic. He is also a graduate of the Massey University Life Writing Course. He has contributed to a number of short story anthologies and journals, including *The Magpie Stole My Heart*, and has had work accepted by Radio New Zealand.

He has children and grandchildren in Abu Dhabi, Rome, Brisbane and Kuala Lumpur and lives with his wife Sue, in Petone near Wellington.